MAX notes®

William Shakespeare's

Richard II

Text by
Michael Morrison
(Ph.D., CUNY)
Department of English
DeVry Institute
Woodbridge, New Jersey

Illustrations by
Arnold Turovskiy

Research & Education Association

MAXnotes® for
RICHARD II

Copyright © 1996 by Research & Education
Association. All rights reserved. No part of this
book may be reproduced in any form without
permission of the publisher.

Printed in the United States of America

Library of Congress Catalog Card Number 96-67421

International Standard Book Number 0-87891-043-3

MAXnotes® is a registered trademark of
Research & Education Association, Piscataway, New Jersey 08854

What **MAXnotes**® *Will Do for You*

This book is intended to help you absorb the essential contents and features of William Shakespeare's *Richard II* and to help you gain a thorough understanding of the work. The book has been designed to do this more quickly and effectively than any other study guide.

For best results, this **MAXnotes** book should be used as a companion to the actual work, not instead of it. The interaction between the two will greatly benefit you.

To help you in your studies, this book presents the most up-to-date interpretations of every section of the actual work, followed by questions and fully explained answers that will enable you to analyze the material critically. The questions also will help you to test your understanding of the work and will prepare you for discussions and exams.

Meaningful illustrations are included to further enhance your understanding and enjoyment of the literary work. The illustrations are designed to place you into the mood and spirit of the work's settings.

The **MAXnotes** also include summaries, character lists, explanations of plot, and section-by-section analyses. A biography of the author and discussion of the work's historical context will help you put this literary piece into the proper perspective of what is taking place.

The use of this study guide will save you the hours of preparation time that would ordinarily be required to arrive at a complete grasp of this work of literature. You will be well prepared for classroom discussions, homework, and exams. The guidelines that are included for writing papers and reports on various topics will prepare you for any added work which may be assigned.

The **MAXnotes** will take your grades "to the max."

Dr. Max Fogiel
Program Director

Contents

> **Each Scene includes List of Characters, Summary, Analysis, Study Questions and Answers, and Suggested Essay Topics.**

SECTION ONE

Introduction

The Life and Work of William Shakespeare

The details of William Shakespeare's life are sketchy, mostly mere surmise based upon court or other clerical records. His parents, John and Mary (Arden), were married about 1557; she was of the landed gentry, and he was a yeoman—a glover and commodities merchant. By 1568, John had risen through the ranks of town government and held the position of high bailiff, which was a position similar to mayor. William, the eldest son and the third of eight children, was born in 1564, probably on April 23, several days before his baptism on April 26 in Stratford-upon-Avon. Shakespeare is also believed to have died on the same date—April 23—in 1616.

It is believed that William attended the local grammar school in Stratford where his parents lived, and that he studied primarily Latin, rhetoric, logic, and literature. Shakespeare probably left school at age 15, which was the norm, to take a job, especially since this was the period of his father's financial difficulty. At age 18 (1582), William married Anne Hathaway, a local farmer's daughter who was eight years his senior. Their first daughter (Susanna) was born six months later (1583), and twins Judith and Hamnet were born in 1585.

Shakespeare's life can be divided into three periods: the first 20 years in Stratford, which include his schooling, early marriage, and fatherhood; the next 25 years as an actor and playwright in London; and the last five in retirement in Stratford where he enjoyed moderate wealth gained from his theatrical successes. The years linking the first two periods are marked by a lack of information about Shakespeare, and are often referred to as the "dark years."

At some point during the "dark years," Shakespeare began his career with a London theatrical company, perhaps in 1589, for he was already an actor and playwright of some note by 1592. Shakespeare apparently wrote and acted for numerous theatrical companies, including Pembroke's Men, and Strange's Men, which later became the Chamberlain's Men, with whom he remained for the rest of his career.

In 1592, the Plague closed the theaters for about two years, and Shakespeare turned to writing book-length narrative poetry. Most notable were *Venus and Adonis* and *The Rape of Lucrece*, both of which were dedicated to the Earl of Southampton, whom scholars accept as Shakespeare's friend and benefactor despite a lack of documentation. During this same period, Shakespeare was writing his sonnets, which are more likely signs of the time's fashion rather than actual love poems detailing any particular relationship. He returned to playwriting when theaters reopened in 1594, and did not continue to write poetry. His sonnets were published without his consent in 1609, shortly before his retirement.

Amid all of his success, Shakespeare suffered the loss of his only son, Hamnet, who died in 1596 at the age of 11. But Shakespeare's career continued unabated, and in London in 1599, he became one of the partners in the new Globe Theater, which was built by the Chamberlain's Men.

Shakespeare wrote very little after 1612, which was the year he completed *Henry VIII*. It was during a performance of this play in 1613 that the Globe caught fire and burned to the ground. Sometime between 1610 and 1613, Shakespeare returned to Stratford, where he owned a large house and property, to spend his remaining years with his family.

William Shakespeare died on April 23, 1616, and was buried two days later in the chancel of Holy Trinity Church, where he had been baptized exactly 52 years earlier. His literary legacy included 37 plays, 154 sonnets, and five major poems.

Incredibly, most of Shakespeare's plays had never been published in anything except pamphlet form, and were simply extant as acting scripts stored at the Globe. Theater scripts were not regarded as literary works of art, but only the basis for the performance. Plays were simply a popular form of entertainment for all layers of society in Shakespeare's time. Only the efforts of two of Shakespeare's company, John Heminges and Henry Condell, preserved his 36 plays (minus *Pericles*, the thirty-seventh).

Shakespeare's Language

Shakespeare's language can create a strong pang of intimidation, even fear, in a large number of modern-day readers. Fortunately, however, this need not be the case. All that is needed to master the art of reading Shakespeare is to practice the techniques of unraveling uncommonly-structured sentences and to become familiar with the poetic use of uncommon words. We must realize that during the 400-year span between Shakespeare's time and our own, both the way we live and speak has changed. Although most of his vocabulary is in use today, some of it is obsolete, and what may be most confusing is that some of his words are used today, but with slightly different or totally different meanings. On the stage, actors readily dissolve these language stumbling blocks. They study Shakespeare's dialogue and express it dramatically in word and in action so that its meaning is graphically enacted. If the reader studies Shakespeare's lines as an actor does, looking up and reflecting upon the meaning of unfamiliar words until real voice is discovered, he or she will suddenly experience the excitement, the depth, and the sheer poetry of what these characters say.

Shakespeare's Sentences

In English, or any other language, the meaning of a sentence greatly depends upon where each word is placed in that sentence. "The child hurt the mother" and "The mother hurt the child" have opposite meanings, even though the words are the same, simply because the words are arranged differently. Because word position is so integral to English, the reader will find unfamiliar word arrangements confusing, even difficult to understand. Since Shakespeare's plays are poetic dramas, he often shifts from average word arrangements to the strikingly unusual so that the line will conform to the desired poetic rhythm. Often, too, Shakespeare employs unusual word order to afford a character his own specific style of speaking.

Today, English sentence structure follows a sequence of subject first, verb second, and an optional object third. Shakespeare, however, often places the verb before the subject, which reads, "Speaks he" rather than "He speaks." Solanio speaks with this inverted structure in *The Merchant of Venice* stating, "I should be still/ Plucking the grass to know where sits the wind" (Bevington edition, I, i, ll.17-19), while today's standard English word order would have the clause at the end of this line read, "where the wind sits." "Wind" is the subject of this clause, and "sits" is the verb. Bassanio's words in Act Two also exemplify this inversion: "And in such eyes as ours appear not faults" (II, ii, l. 184). In our normal word order, we would say, "Faults do not appear in eyes such as ours," with "faults" as the subject in both Shakespeare's word order and ours.

Inversions like these are not troublesome, but when Shakespeare positions the predicate adjective or the object before the subject and verb, we are sometimes surprised. For example, rather than "I saw him," Shakespeare may use a structure such as "Him I saw." Similarly, "Cold the morning is" would be used for our "The morning is cold." Lady Macbeth demonstrates this inversion as she speaks of her husband: "Glamis thou art, and Cawdor, and shalt be/What thou art promised" (*Macbeth*, I, v, ll. 14-15). In current English word order, this quote would begin, "Thou art Glamis, and Cawdor."

In addition to inversions, Shakespeare purposefully keeps words apart that we generally keep together. To illustrate, consider Bassanio's humble admission in *The Merchant of Venice*: "I owe you much, and, like a wilful youth,/That which I owe is lost" (I, i, ll. 146-147). The phrase, "like a wilful youth," separates the regular sequence of "I owe you much" and "That which I owe is lost." To understand more clearly this type of passage, the reader could rearrange these word groups into our conventional order: I owe you much and I wasted what you gave me because I was young and impulsive. While these rearranged clauses will sound like normal English, and will be simpler to understand, they will no longer have the desired poetic rhythm, and the emphasis will now be on the wrong words.

As we read Shakespeare, we will find words that are separated by long, interruptive statements. Often subjects are separated from verbs, and verbs are separated from objects. These long interruptions can be used to give a character dimension or to add an element of suspense. For example, in *Romeo and Juliet* Benvolio describes both Romeo's moodiness and his own sensitive and thoughtful nature:

> I, measuring his affections by my own,
> Which then most sought, where most might not be found,
> Being one too many by my weary self,
> Pursu'd my humour, not pursuing his,
> And gladly shunn'd who gladly fled from me.
> (I, i, ll. 126-130)

In this passage, the subject "I" is distanced from its verb "Pursu'd." The long interruption serves to provide information which is integral to the plot. Another example, taken from *Hamlet,* is the ghost, Hamlet's father, who describes Hamlet's uncle, Claudius, as

> ...that incestuous, that adulterate beast,
> With witchcraft of his wit, with traitorous gifts—
> O wicked wit and gifts, that have the power
> So to seduce—won to his shameful lust
> The will of my most seeming virtuous queen.
> (I, v, ll. 43-47)

From this we learn that Prince Hamlet's mother is the victim of an evil seduction and deception. The delay between the subject, "beast," and the verb, "won," creates a moment of tension filled with the image of a cunning predator waiting for the right moment to spring into attack. This interruptive passage allows the play to unfold crucial information and thus to build the tension necessary to produce a riveting drama.

While at times these long delays are merely for decorative purposes, they are often used to narrate a particular situation or to enhance character development. As *Antony and Cleopatra* opens, an interruptive passage occurs in the first few lines. Although the delay is not lengthy, Philo's words vividly portray Antony's military prowess while they also reveal the immediate concern of the drama.

Antony is distracted from his career and is now focused on Cleopatra:

> ...those goodly eyes,
> That o'er the files and musters of the war
> Have glow'd like plated Mars, now bend, now turn
> The office and devotion of their view
> Upon a tawny front.... (I, i, ll. 2-6)

Whereas Shakespeare sometimes heaps detail upon detail, his sentences are often elliptical, that is, they omit words we expect in written English sentences. In fact, we often do this in our spoken conversations. For instance, we say, "You see that?" when we really mean, "Did you see that?" Reading poetry or listening to lyrics in music conditions us to supply the omitted words and it makes us more comfortable reading this type of dialogue. Consider one passage in *The Merchant of Venice* where Antonio's friends ask him why he seems so sad and Solanio tells Antonio, "Why, then you are in love" (I, i, l. 46). When Antonio denies this, Solanio responds, "Not in love neither?" (I, i, l. 47). The word "you" is omitted but understood despite the confusing double negative.

In addition to leaving out words, Shakespeare often uses intentionally vague language, a strategy which taxes the reader's attentiveness. In *Antony and Cleopatra*, Cleopatra, upset that Antony is leaving for Rome after learning that his wife died in battle, convinces him to stay in Egypt:

> Sir, you and I must part, but that's not it:
> Sir you and I have lov'd, but there's not it;
> That you know well, something it is I would—
> O, my oblivion is a very Antony,
> And I am all forgotten.
> (I, iii, ll. 87-91, emphasis added)

In line 89, "...something it is I would" suggests that there is something that she would want to say, do, or have done. The intentional vagueness leaves us, and certainly Antony, to wonder. Though this sort of writing may appear lackadaisical for all that it leaves out, here the vagueness functions to portray Cleopatra as rhetorically sophisticated. Similarly, when asked what thing a crocodile is (meaning Antony himself who is being compared to a crocodile), Antony slyly evades the question by giving a vague reply:

> It is shap'd, sir, like itself, and it is as broad as it hath breadth. It is just so high as it is, and moves with it own organs. It lives by that which nourisheth it, and, the elements once out of it, it transmigrates.
> (II, vii, ll. 43-46)

This kind of evasiveness, or double-talk, occurs often in Shakespeare's writing and requires extra patience on the part of the reader.

Shakespeare's Words

As we read Shakespeare's plays, we will encounter uncommon words. Many of these words are not in use today. As *Romeo and Juliet* opens, we notice words like "shrift" (confession) and "holidame" (a holy relic). Words like these should be explained in notes to the text. Shakespeare also employs words which we still use, though with different meaning. For example, in *The Merchant of Venice* "caskets" refer to small, decorative chests for holding jewels. However, modern readers may think of a large cask instead of the smaller, diminutive casket.

Another trouble modern readers will have with Shakespeare's English is with words that are still in use today, but which mean something different in Elizabethan use. In *The Merchant of Venice*, Shakespeare uses the word "straight" (as in "straight away") where we would say "immediately." Here, the modern reader is unlikely to carry away the wrong message, however, since the modern meaning will simply make no sense. In this case, textual notes will clarify a phrase's meaning. To cite another example, in *Romeo and Juliet*, after Mercutio dies, Romeo states that the "black fate on moe days doth depend" (emphasis added). In this case, "depend" really means "impend."

Shakespeare's Wordplay

All of Shakespeare's works exhibit his mastery of playing with language and with such variety that many people have authored entire books on this subject alone. Shakespeare's most frequently used types of wordplay are common: metaphors, similes, synecdoche and metonymy, personification, allusion, and puns. It is when Shakespeare violates the normal use of these devices, or rhetorical figures, that the language becomes confusing.

A metaphor is a comparison in which an object or idea is replaced by another object or idea with common attributes. For example, in *Macbeth* a murderer tells Macbeth that Banquo has been murdered, as directed, but that his son, Fleance, escaped, having witnessed his father's murder. Fleance, now a threat to Macbeth, is described as a serpent:

> There the grown serpent lies, the worm that's fled
> Hath nature that in time will venom breed,
> No teeth for the present. (III, iv, ll. 29-31, emphasis added)

Similes, on the other hand, compare objects or ideas while using the words "like" or "as." In *Romeo and Juliet*, Romeo tells Juliet that "Love goes toward love as schoolboys from their books" (II, ii, l. 156). Such similes often give way to more involved comparisons, "extended similes." For example, Juliet tells Romeo:

> 'Tis almost morning, I would have thee gone,
> And yet no farther than a wonton's bird,
> That lets it hop a little from his hand
> Like a poor prisoner in his twisted gyves,
> And with silken thread plucks it back again,
> So loving-jealous of his liberty.
> (II, ii, ll. 176-181, emphasis added)

An epic simile, a device borrowed from heroic poetry, is an extended simile that builds into an even more elaborate comparison. In *Macbeth*, Macbeth describes King Duncan's virtues with an angelic, celestial simile and then drives immediately into another simile that redirects us into a vision of warfare and destruction:

> ...Besides this Duncan
> Hath borne his faculties so meek, hath been
> So clear in his great office, that his virtues
> Will plead like angels, trumpet-tongued, against
> The deep damnation of his taking-off;
> And pity, like a naked new-born babe,
> Striding the blast, or heaven's cherubim, horsed
> Upon the sightless couriers of the air,
> Shall blow the horrid deed in every eye,
> That tears shall drown the wind....
> (I, vii, ll. 16-25, emphasis added)

Shakespeare employs other devices, like synecdoche and metonymy, to achieve "verbal economy," or using one or two words to express more than one thought. Synecdoche is a figure of speech using a part for the whole. An example of synecdoche is using the word boards to imply a stage. Boards are only a small part of the materials that make up a stage, however, the term boards has become a colloquial synonym for stage. Metonymy is a figure of speech using the name of one thing for that of another which it is associated. An example of metonymy is using crown to mean the king (as used in the sentence "These lands belong to the crown"). Since a crown is associated with or an attribute of the king, the word crown has become a metonymy for the king. It is important to understand that every metonymy is a synecdoche, but not every synecdoche is a metonymy. This rule is true because a metonymy must not only be a part of the root word, making a synecdoche, but also be a unique attribute of or associated with the root word.

Synecdoche and metonymy in Shakespeare's works is often very confusing to a new student because he creates uses for words that they usually do not perform. This technique is often complicated and yet very subtle, which makes it difficult for a new student to dissect and understand. An example of these devices in one of Shakespeare's plays can be found in *The Merchant of Venice*. In warning his daughter, Jessica, to ignore the Christian revelries in the streets below, Shylock says:

Lock up my doors; and when you hear the drum
And the vile squealing of the wry-necked fife,
Clamber not you up to the casements then...
(I, v, ll. 30-32)

The phrase of importance in this quote is "the wry-necked fife."
When a reader examines this phrase it does not seem to make
sense; a fife is a cylinder-shaped instrument, there is no part of it
that can be called a neck. The phrase then must be taken to refer
to the fife-player, who has to twist his or her neck to play the fife.
Fife, therefore, is a synecdoche for fife-player, much as boards is
for stage. The trouble with understanding this phrase is that "vile
squealing" logically refers to the sound of the fife, not the fife-
player, and the reader might be led to take fife as the instrument
because of the parallel reference to "drum" in the previous line.
The best solution to this quandary is that Shakespeare uses the
word fife to refer to both the instrument and the player. Both the
player and the instrument are needed to complete the wordplay
in this phrase, which, though difficult to understand to new readers, cannot be seen as a flaw since Shakespeare manages to
convey two meanings with one word. This remarkable example
of synecdoche illuminates Shakespeare's mastery of "verbal
economy."

Shakespeare also uses vivid and imagistic wordplay through
personification, in which human capacities and behaviors are at-
tributed to inanimate objects. Bassanio, in *The Merchant of Venice*,
almost speechless when Portia promises to marry him and share
all her worldly wealth, states "my blood speaks to you in my veins..."
(III, ii, l. 176). How deeply he must feel since even his blood can
speak. Similarly, Portia, learning of the penalty that Antonio must
pay for defaulting on his debt, tells Salerio, "There are some shrewd
contents in yond same paper/That steals the color from Bassanio's
cheek" (III, ii, ll. 243-244).

Another important facet of Shakespeare's rhetorical repertoire
is his use of allusion. An allusion is a reference to another author
or to an historical figure or event. Very often Shakespeare alludes
to the heroes and heroines of Ovid's *Metamorphoses*. For example,

in Cymbeline an entire room is decorated with images illustrating the stories from this classical work, and the heroine, Imogen, has been reading from this text. Similarly, in *Titus Andronicus* characters not only read directly from the *Metamorphoses*, but a subplot re-enacts one of the *Metamorphoses's* most famous stories, the rape and mutilation of Philomel.

Another way Shakespeare uses allusion is to drop names of mythological, historical, and literary figures. In *The Taming of the Shrew*, for instance, Petruchio compares Katharina, the woman whom he is courting, to Diana (II, i, l. 55), the virgin goddess, in order to suggest that Katharina is a man-hater. At times, Shakespeare will allude to well-known figures without so much as mentioning their names. In *Twelfth Night*, for example, though the Duke and Valentine are ostensibly interested in Olivia, a rich countess, Shakespeare asks his audience to compare the Duke's emotional turmoil to the plight of Acteon, whom the goddess Diana transforms into a deer to be hunted and killed by Acteon's own dogs:

Duke: That instant was I turn'd into a hart,
           And my desires, like fell and cruel hounds,
           E'er since pursue me.
           [...]
Valentine: But like a cloistress she will veiled walk,
           And water once a day her chamber round....
           (I, i, l. 20 ff.)

Shakespeare's use of puns spotlights his exceptional wit. His comedies in particular are loaded with puns, usually of a sexual nature. Puns work through the ambiguity that results when multiple senses of a word are evoked; homophones often cause this sort of ambiguity. In *Antony and Cleopatra*, Enobarbus believes "there is mettle in death" (I, ii, l. 146), meaning that there is "courage" in death; at the same time, mettle suggests the homophone metal, referring to swords made of metal causing death. In early editions of Shakespeare's work there was no distinction made between the two words. Antony puns on the word "earing," (I, ii, ll. 112-114) meaning both plowing (as in rooting out weeds) and hearing: he angrily sends away a messenger, not wishing to hear the message from his wife, Fulvia: "...O then we bring forth weeds,/ when our quick minds lie still, and our ills told us/Is as our earing." If ill-natured news is planted in one's "hearing," it will render an "earing" (harvest) of ill-natured thoughts. A particularly clever pun, also in *Antony and Cleopatra,* stands out after Antony's troops have fought Octavius's men in Egypt: "We have beat him to his camp. Run one before,/And let the queen know of our gests" (IV, viii, ll. 1-2). Here "gests" means deeds (in this case, deeds of battle); it is also a pun on "guests," as though Octavius' slain soldiers were to be guests when buried in Egypt.

One should note that Elizabethan pronunciation was in several cases different from our own. Thus, modern readers, especially Americans, will miss out on the many puns based on homophones. The textual notes will point out many of these "lost" puns, however.

Shakespeare's sexual innuendoes can be either clever or tedious depending upon the speaker and situation. The modern reader should recall that sexuality in Shakespeare's time was far more complex than in ours and that characters may refer to such things as masturbation and homosexual activity. Textual notes in some editions will point out these puns but rarely explain them. An example of a sexual pun or innuendo can be found in *The Merchant of Venice* when Portia and Nerissa are discussing Portia's past suitors using innuendo to tell of their sexual prowess:

> Portia: I pray thee, overname them, and as thou
>   namest them, I will describe them, and
>   according to my description level at my
>   affection.
> Nerissa: First, there is the Neapolitan prince.
> Portia: Ay, that's a colt indeed, for he doth nothing but
>   talk of his horse, and he makes it a great
>   appropriation to his own good parts that he can
>   shoe him himself. I am much afeard my lady his
>   mother played false with the smith.
>   (I, ii, ll. 35-45)

The "Neapolitan prince" is given a grade of an inexperienced youth when Portia describes him as a "colt." The prince is thought to be inexperienced because he did nothing but "talk of his horse" (a pun for his penis) and his other great attributes. Portia goes on to say that the prince boasted that he could "shoe him [his horse] himself," a possible pun meaning that the prince was very proud that he could masturbate. Finally, Portia makes an attack upon the prince's mother, saying that "my lady his mother played false with the smith," a pun to say his mother must have committed adultery with a blacksmith to give birth to such a vulgar man having an obsession with "shoeing his horse."

It is worth mentioning that Shakespeare gives the reader hints when his characters might be using puns and innuendoes. In *The Merchant of Venice*, Portia's lines are given in prose when she is joking, or engaged in bawdy conversations. Later on the reader will notice that Portia's lines are rhymed in poetry, such as when she is talking in court or to Bassanio. This is Shakespeare's way of letting the reader know when Portia is jesting and when she is serious.

Shakespeare's Dramatic Verse

Finally, the reader will notice that some lines are actually rhymed verse while others are in verse without rhyme; and much of Shakespeare's drama is in prose. Shakespeare usually has his lovers speak in the language of love poetry which uses rhymed couplets. The archetypal example of this comes, of course, from *Romeo and Juliet*:

> The grey-ey'd morn smiles on the frowning night,
> Check'ring the eastern clouds with streaks of light,
> And fleckled darkness like a drunkard reels
> From forth day's path and Titan's fiery wheels.
> (II, iii, ll. 1-4)

Here it is ironic that Friar Lawrence should speak these lines since he is not the one in love. He, therefore, appears buffoonish and out of touch with reality. Shakespeare often has his characters speak in rhymed verse to let the reader know that the character is acting in jest, and vice-versa.

Perhaps the majority of Shakespeare's lines are in blank verse, a form of poetry which does not use rhyme (hence the name blank)

but still employs a rhythm native to the English language, iambic
pentameter, where every second syllable in a line of ten syllables
receives stress. Consider the following verses from *Hamlet*, and
note the accents and the lack of end-rhyme:

> The síngle ánd pecúliar lífe is bóund
> With áll the stréngth and ármor óf the mínd
> (III, iii, ll. 12-13)

The final syllable of these verses receives stress and is said to
have a hard, or "strong," ending. A soft ending, also said to be
"weak," receives no stress. In *The Tempest*, Shakespeare uses a soft
ending to shape a verse that demonstrates through both sound
(meter) and sense the capacity of the feminine to propagate:

> and thén I lóv'd thee
> And shów'd thee áll the quálitíes o' th' ísle,
> The frésh spríngs, bríne-pits, bárren pláce and fértile.
> (I, ii, ll. 338-40)

The first and third of these lines here have soft endings.

In general, Shakespeare saves blank verse for his characters of
noble birth. Therefore, it is significant when his lofty characters
speak in prose. Prose holds a special place in Shakespeare's dia-
logues; he uses it to represent the speech habits of the common
people. Not only do lowly servants and common citizens speak in
prose, but important, lower class figures also use this fun, at times
ribald variety of speech. Though Shakespeare crafts some very or-
nate lines in verse, his prose can be equally daunting, for some of
his characters may speechify and break into double-talk in their
attempts to show sophistication. A clever instance of this comes
when the Third Citizen in *Coriolanus* refers to the people's para-
doxical lack of power when they must elect Coriolanus as their new
leader once Coriolanus has orated how he has courageously fought
for them in battle:

> We have power in ourselves to do it, but it is
> a power that we have no power to do; for if he show us his
> wounds and tell us his deeds, we are to put our tongues into

those wounds and speak for them; so, if he tell us his noble
deeds, we must also tell him our noble acceptance of them.
Ingratitude is monstrous, and for the multitude to be
ingrateful were to make a monster of the multitude, of the
which we, being members, should bring ourselves to be
monstrous members.
(II, ii, ll. 3-13)

Notice that this passage contains as many metaphors, hideous
though they be, as any other passage in Shakespeare's dramatic verse.

When reading Shakespeare, paying attention to characters who
suddenly break into rhymed verse, or who slip into prose after
speaking in blank verse, will heighten your awareness of a
character's mood and personal development. For instance, in
Antony and Cleopatra, the famous military leader Marcus Antony
usually speaks in blank verse, but also speaks in fits of prose (II, iii,
ll. 43-46) once his masculinity and authority have been questioned.
Similarly, in *Timon of Athens*, after the wealthy Lord Timon abandons the city of Athens to live in a cave, he harangues anyone whom
he encounters in prose (IV, iii, l. 331 ff.). In contrast, the reader
should wonder why the bestial Caliban in *The Tempest* speaks in
blank verse rather than in prose.

Implied Stage Action

When we read a Shakespearean play, we are reading a performance text. Actors interact through dialogue, but at the same time
these actors cry, gesticulate, throw tantrums, pick up daggers, and
compulsively wash murderous "blood" from their hands. Some of
the action that takes place on stage is explicitly stated in stage directions. However, some of the stage activity is couched within the
dialogue itself. Attentiveness to these cues is important as one con-
ceives how to visualize the action. When Iago in *Othello* feigns concern for Cassio whom he himself has stabbed, he calls to the
surrounding men, "Come, come:/Lend me a light" (V, i, ll. 86-87). It
is almost sure that one of the actors involved will bring him a torch
or lantern. In the same play, Emilia, Desdemona's maidservant, asks
if she should fetch her lady's nightgown and Desdemona replies,
"No, unpin me here" (IV, iii, l. 37). In *Macbeth*, after killing Duncan,

Macbeth brings the murder weapon back with him. When he tells his wife that he cannot return to the scene and place the daggers to suggest that the king's guards murdered Duncan, she castigates him: "Infirm of purpose/Give me the daggers. The sleeping and the dead are but as pictures" (II, ii, ll. 50-52). As she exits, it is easy to visualize Lady Macbeth grabbing the daggers from her husband.

For 400 years, readers have found it greatly satisfying to work with all aspects of Shakespeare's language—the implied stage action, word choice, sentence structure, and wordplay—until all aspects come to life. Just as seeing a fine performance of a Shakespearean play is exciting, staging the play in one's own mind's eye, and revisiting lines to enrich the sense of the action, will enhance one's appreciation of Shakespeare's extraordinary literary and dramatic achievements.

Historical Background

Richard II was probably written and first performed in 1595. Shakespeare's principal source for the play was the second edition of Raphael Holinshed's *Chronicles of England, Scotland and Ireland*, published in 1587. Shakespeare may also have drawn from a number of additional sources including an anonymous play entitled *Thomas of Woodstock*, Jean Froissart's *Chronicles* (1525), Edward Halle's *The Union of the Two Noble and Illustre Families of Lancaster and York* (1548), *A Mirror for Magistrates* (1559), Samuel Daniel's *The Civil Wars* (1595), and three French manuscript accounts of King Richard's reign. It is possible, as well, that Shakespeare was influenced by Christopher Marlowe's *Edward II* (c. 1593). This play, like *Richard II*, also deals with a monarch who is ill-suited to govern and ultimately abdicates the throne.

The story Shakespeare tells in *Richard II* precedes those told in *Henry IV, Parts I and II* and *Henry V*. The last three plays, which continue the saga of the House of Lancaster, were written and produced between 1597 and 1599. It is likely that Shakespeare had a series of plays in mind when he wrote *Richard II*, for he had earlier written a four-part cycle of English chronicle plays comprising the *Henry VI* trilogy and *Richard III*.

The reign of the historical Richard II took place between 1377 and 1399; the events depicted in Shakespeare's play cover only the last two years of his kingship and his death in February of 1400. Thus, Shakespeare was looking back on the events of two centuries earlier. Richard II was the grandson of King Edward III and the son of Edward the Black Prince, both noted patriots and warriors. The Black Prince, eldest of Edward II's seven sons, died at age 46 in 1376, and Richard, upon his grandfather's death a year later, ascended the throne at the age of ten. The practical details of government were overseen by a series of councils until 1389, when Richard, at 22, declared himself of age to govern.

The age of Richard II was noteworthy for the flourishing of English literature; Geoffrey Chaucer, one of the first great English poets, held royal administrative posts and served in Parliament during Richard's reign. Richard had little success, however, as a politician. He was unable to reconcile rivalries among his nobles and showed little interest in an ongoing war with France. In addition, he achieved widespread unpopularity among the nobles and commoners for his imperious style of government. Generally considered a weak king, he was deposed in 1399 in a rebellion led by his cousin Henry Bolingbroke, Duke of Hereford, who later became King Henry IV.

Critics generally agree that *Richard II* is a significant milestone in Shakespeare's artistic development. At the time Shakespeare wrote *Richard II* he had been a playwright for about six years, yet his great tragedies were still to come. A probing meditation on the nature and responsibilities of kingship, it is the first play he wrote in which the protagonist is an eloquent, introspective man of poetic imagination. The play is noteworthy, as well, for the lyrical beauty of its verse, and for its remarkable portrait of a king whose tragic flaws lead to his own downfall.

The many printed editions which appeared within a few years of its initial production attest to the popularity of this play in Shakespeare's time. The First Quarto of *Richard II* appeared in 1597. This edition proved popular enough to warrant two additional printings the following year and another two before Shakespeare's death.

In early editions, however, it was necessary to omit the deposition scene. At the time *Richard II* was first published, Elizabeth I was in her mid-sixties and without an heir. The line of succession was very much in question. Not until 1608, when James I was securely on the throne, was this scene allowed to be printed by government censors, although it is likely that the deposition was performed regularly in the stage version.

This scene, in fact, aroused considerable controversy when it was staged on the eve of an abortive uprising against the English monarchy. In early February of 1601, a delegation of noblemen approached Shakespeare's company and offered to pay a substantial fee for a special performance of *Richard II* at the Globe Theatre. The play was performed without incident on February 7, but the next day the Earl of Essex, formerly a favorite of Queen Elizabeth, mounted a rebellion against the crown. As a subsequent inquest revealed, Essex's followers had specifically requested a performance of *Richard II* because it featured a scene of a monarch's deposition. The rebellion was quickly suppressed. Essex was captured. He was beheaded three weeks later.

At the inquest, Shakespeare's company was found to be innocent of any wrongdoing. In fact, the company performed for the Queen at Whitehall Palace on the eve of Essex's execution. In August of that year, William Lambarde, an archivist at the Tower of London, recorded Queen Elizabeth's only known comments on one of Shakespeare's plays: "I am Richard the Second, know ye not that?... This tragedy was played forty times in open streets and houses."

In the four centuries since it was first produced, *Richard II* has enjoyed a rich and colorful stage history. We have records of a performance on September 30, 1607 acted by crew members of the H. M. S. *Dragon* off the coast of Sierra Leone. We also have records of a production at the Globe in 1631, fifteen years after Shakespeare's death. In 1681, *Richard II* was adapted for production by Nahum Tate. The play was retitled *The Sicilian Usurper* and the names of the characters were changed. However the theme of regicide still aroused controversy and the play was suppressed after a few performances. In 1719, another adaptation was produced in London, and in 1738 Shakespeare's original was restored to the stage at Covent Garden.

A notable early nineteenth-century performance of *Richard II* was that given by the brilliant and mercurial English actor Edmund

Kean. Kean's portrayal, first seen in London in 1815, was successful with critics and the public and the play remained in his repertory for the next thirteen years. In 1857, Charles Kean, Edmund's son, offered London playgoers a spectacular revival featuring hundreds of extras, real horses on stage, historically accurate costumes, and lavish interpolated pageantry. His revival played for 85 performances, a record at the time.

One of the most interesting events in the play's performance history came on April 23, 1879, Shakespeare's birthday. That evening, Edwin Booth, the great American tragedian and brother of John Wilkes Booth, who fourteen years earlier had assassinated Abraham Lincoln at Ford's Theatre in Washington, was playing Richard II at McVicker's Theatre in Chicago. As Booth was giving Richard's soliloquy in the fifth act, a madman stood up in the balcony, raised a gun, and fired one shot, then another, as Booth sat alone on stage. The bullets narrowly missed Booth, who pointed to the gunman and cried, "Arrest that man." The potential assassin was subdued and was later confined to an asylum. Booth, after calming the audience and comforting his wife backstage, returned to finish the performance. Afterwards, he had one of the bullets pried out of the scenery where it had lodged, mounted it in a gold cartridge, and wore it on his watch chain for the rest of his life.

In the twentieth century, the role of Richard II has attracted a number of leading actors. The English actor-managers Frank Benson and Herbert Beerbohm Tree mounted productions in London just after the turn of the century. Tree's production was given several subsequent West End stagings, and Benson revived the play regularly for the next decade at the Shakespeare festival he directed at Stratford-upon-Avon. John Gielgud played an acclaimed Richard II at the Old Vic in London in 1929, and he reprised the role at the Queen's Theatre in 1937. The English actor Maurice Evans performed Richard II on Broadway that same year in a well-received production directed by Margaret Webster.

During the 1950s and 60s, the role of Shakespeare's introspective poet-king found notable interpreters in Paul Scofield, David Warner, and Ian McKellen. In 1973, John Barton staged a critically praised production for England's Royal Shakespeare Company with Richard Pasco and Ian Richardson alternating as Richard and

Bolingbroke. Noteworthy revivals in recent years include Ariane Mnouchkine's stylized production in France in 1981, which subsequently played in Los Angeles, and the 1994 New York Shakespeare Festival production directed by Steven Berkoff. In 1995, the Irish actress Fiona Shaw attempted the role of Richard at the National Theatre of Great Britain in London and was received enthusiastically by audiences and critics.

Master List of Characters

King Richard II—*King of England and grandson of the late King Edward III.*

Edmund, Duke of York—*Son of the late King Edward III; uncle to Richard II and Henry Bolingbroke and father of the Duke of Aumerle.*

John of Gaunt, Duke of Lancaster—*Another son of the late King Edward III; uncle to Richard II and father of Henry Bolingbroke.*

Henry Bolingbroke, Duke of Hereford—*John of Gaunt's son and cousin to Richard II; later King Henry IV.*

The Duke of Aumerle—*Son of Edmund, Duke of York; cousin to Richard II and Henry Bolingbroke.*

Thomas Mowbray, Duke of Norfolk—*A nobleman who is accused of treason by Henry Bolingbroke.*

The Earl of Salisbury—*An ally of King Richard II who commands the English army when Richard is in Ireland.*

The Earl of Berkeley—*A nobleman and ally of the King.*

Sir John Bushy—*A courtier and favorite of King Richard II.*

Sir William Bagot—*Another courtier and royal favorite.*

Sir Henry Green—*A third courtier favored by the King.*

The Earl of Northumberland—*A nobleman who joins Henry Bolingbroke's rebellion against King Richard.*

Harry Percy—*Son of the Earl of Northumberland who joins his father in his alliance with Bolingbroke.*

Lord Ross—*An ally of the Earl of Northumberland who joins in Bolingbroke's rebellion.*

Lord Willoughby—*Another ally of the Earl of Northumberland who joins Bolingbroke's rebellion.*

The Bishop of Carlisle—*A clergyman loyal to King Richard.*

Sir Stephen Scroop—*A soldier and ally of King Richard.*

Lord Fitzwater—*A nobleman who accuses the Duke of Aumerle of treason.*

The Duke of Surrey—*A nobleman who defends the Duke of Aumerle against Fitzwater's charges.*

The Abbot of Westminster—*A clergyman loyal to King Richard who plots against King Henry IV.*

Sir Pierce of Exton—*A knight loyal to King Henry IV; murderer of Richard II.*

Lord Marshal—*A high official at the court of Richard II.*

Welsh Captain—*Commander of the Welsh troops in King Richard's army.*

Queen Isabel—*Second wife to Richard II.*

Duchess of Gloucester—*Sister-in-law to John of Gaunt and the Duke of York; widow of the murdered Duke of Gloucester and aunt by marriage to Richard II.*

Duchess of York—*Wife to Edmund, Duke of York; mother of the Duke of Aumerle.*

Ladies-in-Waiting—*Attendants to the Queen.*

Gardeners—*Servants to the Duke of York.*

A keeper—*Jailer at Pomfret Castle.*

A groom—*Stable hand who tended King Richard's horses.*

Heralds, Lords, Officers, Soldiers, Attendants, and Servants—*Unnamed characters throughout the play, who are only referred to by their military position or through the character it is their job to serve.*

Summary of the Play

King Richard II hears accusations made by his cousin Henry Bolingbroke, Duke of Hereford, that Thomas Mowbray, Duke of Norfolk, has embezzled royal funds and is responsible for the recent murder of the Duke of Gloucester. Mowbray vehemently denies the charges. King Richard, unable to reconcile the contending noblemen, orders that a trial by combat will be held at Coventry to settle the matter.

Before the combat can begin, however, King Richard decides to banish both adversaries, Bolingbroke for ten years, later reduced to six, and Mowbray for life. He then makes plans to lead a military campaign in Ireland. News arrives that John of Gaunt, Bolingbroke's father and Richard's uncle, is grievously ill. The King expresses the hope that Gaunt will die so he can confiscate his estate to finance his Irish wars.

Gaunt, on his deathbed, tells the King that he has surrounded himself with flattering courtiers and has brought England to the brink of financial ruin. Richard, furious, calls his uncle a fool. When news of Gaunt's death arrives, Richard seizes his money and lands for the crown. Soon afterward, the Earl of Northumberland announces that Bolingbroke has set sail for England with an army to claim his inheritance. He and his followers, dissatisfied by Richard's misrule, resolve to join Bolingbroke's cause.

The Duke of York, appointed Lord Governor in Richard's absence, prepares to meet the rebels, but he admits that he is ill-equipped to cope with a military emergency. Bolingbroke explains to York that he has returned to England only to claim the title and estate of his late father. York agrees to remain neutral in the conflict.

King Richard arrives in Wales after his Irish campaign, confident that Bolingbroke's rebellion will be suppressed. Soon afterward, however, he receives bad tidings. Twelve thousand Welsh soldiers in his army have deserted. Bolingbroke has captured and executed two of his favorites, and the common people have sided with Bolingbroke. Even the Duke of York has allied with the rebels. Recognizing the hopelessness of his situation, he resolves to seek refuge at Flint Castle nearby.

Bolingbroke arrives at the castle and vows allegiance to his sovereign if Richard will repeal his banishment and restore his inheritance. Richard appears on the walls of the castle and grants Bolingbroke's demands. Although Bolingbroke has pledged loyalty if Richard capitulates, Richard himself brings up the idea of abdication and agrees to be led to London where the issue of the crown will be formally resolved. Richard's Queen learns of his misfortune from the Duke of York's gardeners.

At the Parliament Hall in London, York announces that Richard has agreed to be deposed in favor of Bolingbroke, who will then be crowned King Henry IV. Richard appears before Parliament and surrenders his crown reluctantly. Bolingbroke orders Richard to be imprisoned and makes plans for his own coronation.

As he is led to prison, Richard bids a sad farewell to his Queen. Alone in his prison cell, he reflects philosophically on his misfortunes. Soon afterward, Sir Pierce of Exton, having overheard King Henry declare his desire to be rid of Richard, arrives with several armed assassins. They enter Richard's cell, and Richard, with a burst of valor, kills two of the men. However, he is outnumbered, and Exton kills the former king. Exton then escorts Richard's coffin to King Henry's throne room. King Henry promptly renounces Richard's murderer. Stricken with guilt, he plans a pilgrimage to the Holy Land to soothe his uneasy conscience.

Estimated Reading Time

This play should take the average student about five hours to read. It will be helpful to divide your reading time into five one-hour sittings for each of the play's five acts. The time may vary, however, depending on the length of each act. Shakespeare's language can be difficult for students who are unfamiliar with it, so each act should be read carefully on a scene-by-scene basis to ensure understanding.

(Note: All line number references in this book refer to the Signet Classic edition. If you are using another edition of the play, line number references may differ slightly.)

SECTION TWO

Act I

Act I, Scene 1

New Characters:

Richard II: *King of England*

John of Gaunt: *Duke of Lancaster; King Richard's uncle and Henry Bolingbroke's father*

Henry Bolingbroke: *Duke of Hereford and son to John of Gaunt; cousin to Richard II*

Thomas Mowbray: *Duke of Norfolk; accused by Bolingbroke of treason*

Summary

Act I, Scene 1 takes place in the throne room at Windsor Castle. The elderly John of Gaunt, Duke of Lancaster, tells the King he has brought his son and heir, Henry Bolingbroke, who wishes to bring formal charges of treason against Thomas Mowbray, Duke of Norfolk. King Richard summons Bolingbroke and Mowbray to his presence: "Face to face,/ And frowning brow to brow, ourselves will hear/ The accuser and the accused freely speak" (15-17).

Bolingbroke and Mowbray enter and greet the King with respectful praise. Richard thanks them, but he comments that "one but flatters us." He then asks to hear Bolingbroke's accusations. Bolingbroke accuses Mowbray of treason, but Mowbray replies vehemently that Bolingbroke is "a slanderous coward and a villain" (61). Bolingbroke responds by throwing down his gage (a glove),

issuing a challenge to a joust by the "rites of knighthood." Mowbray picks up the gage and accepts the challenge.

Bolingbroke then lists the specifics of his charge. He accuses Mowbray of embezzling royal funds designated for the King's army in France and plotting the recent murder of Thomas of Woodstock, Duke of Gloucester, uncle to Bolingbroke and the King. Mowbray calls Bolingbroke a liar; he admits that he once plotted to kill John of Gaunt, but he denies having a part in Gloucester's death and hurls down his gage to assert his innocence. Richard attempts to reconcile the adversaries: "Wrath-kindled gentlemen, be ruled by me;/ Let's purge this choler without letting blood" (152-153).

At the King's request, Gaunt attempts to calm his son and urges him to withdraw his challenge; Richard attempts to calm Mowbray. Bolingbroke and Mowbray refuse to be appeased, however. King Richard then proclaims that the issue will be settled in a trial by combat "At Coventry upon Saint Lambert's day" (199).

Analysis

An important event has taken place prior to the beginning of the play. While imprisoned in the French port of Calais (then a part of England's conquered territory) Thomas of Woodstock, Duke of Gloucester, the youngest brother to Richard's father and John of Gaunt, was murdered in his cell under mysterious circumstances. This incident forms the basis of the quarrel King Richard is asked to arbitrate.

This scene, which features a ceremonious gathering of nobles and attendants, reveals the pageantry and ritual of King Richard's court. The speech throughout is formal; note that many of the characters conclude their declarations with rhymed couplets. Even the most violent sentiments are expressed in ceremonious language. Note, also, that many of the characters make Biblical allusions and utter religious oaths. These references foreshadow subsequent religious imagery and the many ensuing references to the divine right of kings, which later will become one of the play's central themes.

Early in this scene we are greeted by images of the four elements—images that will recur frequently during the course of the play. In the opening lines, there are references to earth (which later will be extended to include soil and gardening), air (also sky and heavens), fire (which also will encompass the sun, an emblem of kingship), and water (Richard, the sun-king, will later clash with Bolingbroke, the flood; there will also be many references to tears). The King, for example, remarks of the contending noblemen: "High-stomached are they both, and full of ire,/ In rage, deaf as the sea, hasty as fire" (18-19). Soon afterward, Mowbray expresses that hope that the King's days will be happy "Until the heavens envying earth's good hap,/ Add an immortal title to your crown" (23-24).

Shakespeare also makes frequent use of blood imagery throughout this scene—another poetic image that will recur throughout the play. Blood is used in two senses, which often overlap: the blood of murder and violent conflict, and the blood of kinship and inheritance. Bolingbroke, for instance, refers to the Duke of Gloucester's blood, as "...like sacrificing Abel's, cries/ ...to me for justice" (104-106) and to "...my high blood's royalty" (71). The true meaning of his words will resonate in scenes to come. Abel, of course, was killed by a member of his own family, and Bolingbroke will later assert more directly the royalty of his lineage. Later in this scene, Richard attempts to settle the quarrel "without letting blood." He comments, with a diplomatic attempt at humor: "Our doctors say this is no month to bleed" (157). This reference, too, will resonate later in the play when Bolingbroke and Mowbray prepare to settle their quarrel on the tilting field in Coventry.

The youthful king (then in his early thirties) revels in the pageantry of his office and his own central role in the proceedings. Throughout, he attempts to maintain a public posture of kingly impartiality; he comments to Mowbray that "Were [Bolingbroke] my brother, nay, my kingdom's heir,/ As he is but my father's brother's son,/ Now by my sceptre's awe I make a vow,/ Such neighbor nearness to our sacred blood/ Shall nothing privilege him nor partialize/ The unstooping firmness of my upright soul" (116-121). He questions the adversaries carefully; indeed, he remains silent and detached through many of their contentious exchanges. Yet earlier we have seen a hint of his private feelings when he observed Bolingbroke's vociferous boldness: "How high a pitch his resolution soars!" (109).

Note that Bolingbroke denounces the murder of Gloucester

with particular vehemence, and that his accusations seem directed as much to the King as to Mowbray. Mowbray's confidence, on the other hand, seems to imply royal support. We learn that he has in the past loaned money to the King. Although he denies that he had a part in Gloucester's murder, he laments that he had "Neglected my sworn duty in that case" (134). The nature of his duty is never explained, however, and there is no clear indication of who is right and who is wrong in the quarrel.

The throwing down of a gage was a traditional Medieval challenge to a duel on horseback with lances and swords—a challenge that must be answered for the sake of honor, and one that usually resulted in the death of one of the combatants. When Richard is unable to pacify the contentious nobles, he proclaims reluctantly that a joust will be held on September 17—St. Lambert's Day—to resolve the issue. It was assumed that God would have a hand in the outcome by assisting the rightful claimant to victory.

When Richard proclaims, "Lions make leopards tame" and "We were not born to sue, but to command," he defines his self-image (174; 196). Indeed, he presides ceremoniously and with serene confidence over the assembled nobles. Yet we are given an indication of his lack of skills as a politician when he fails to successfully arbitrate the Bolingbroke-Mowbray dispute. The contending nobles do not obey his royal decree to throw down their adversaries' gages; significantly, Bolingbroke also refuses to obey his father's request that he respect the King's wishes. Thus, Richard can only settle the matter by ordering the trial by combat Bolingbroke and Mowbray had originally demanded.

Act I, Scene 2

New Character:

Duchess of Gloucester: *sister-in-law to John of Gaunt; widow of the murdered Duke of Gloucester*

Summary

At his palace in London, John of Gaunt attempts to comfort his grieving sister-in-law, the widow of the slain Duke of Gloucester.

He tells her that he, too, is troubled by his brother's murder, and he assures her that the "will of heaven" will "...rain hot vengeance on offenders' heads" (8). However the Duchess, tormented by her husband's death, urges Gaunt to personally avenge her husband. She appeals to Gaunt's sense of brotherly love. She also tells him that "To safeguard thine own life,/ The best way is to venge my Gloucester's death" (35-36). However Gaunt tells the Duchess that her quarrel is with God, for "God's substitute," King Richard, ordered Gloucester's murder. If it was wrong, he remarks, God will avenge it. He tells her firmly that he will "...never lift/ An angry arm against His minister" (40-41).

The Duchess of Gloucester bids Gaunt a reluctant farewell, yet she is still eager for revenge and hopes that Bolingbroke will prevail in his joust with Mowbray. Gaunt takes leave of his sister-in-law and prepares to journey to Coventry, where the joust will take place. Before he departs, the Duchess sends greetings to Edmund, Duke of York, her only surviving brother-in-law besides Gaunt. She invites York to visit her but changes her mind when she realizes her sorrow will make her a poor hostess.

Analysis

This intimate scene stands in sharp contrast to the formal pageantry of Scene 1. Here, we are greeted by a far more human glimpse of the aftermath of Gloucester's death. In the first scene, the murder of Gloucester was a political issue; in this scene, it is more personal.

In the most significant revelation of Scene 2, we learn that King Richard is responsible for Gloucester's assassination. The Duchess is eager for revenge, yet Gaunt tells her that only "the will of heaven" can provide justice. When Gaunt refers to Richard as "God's substitute" we are introduced directly to one of the play's many themes: the divine right of kings. This doctrine was widely accepted in Medieval and Renaissance England. It was assumed that monarchs ruled with sacred authority. Thus, Gaunt feels helpless to take vengeful action against his sovereign, for to do so would be to rebel against God Himself. The disparity between the notion that Richard rules as "God's annointed" and his capricious and irresponsible behavior as King will provide one of the central conflicts of the play.

This scene contrasts the contradictory desires for patience and revenge; we are also greeted by frequent reprises of the blood imagery from Scene 1. The Duchess, for example, refers to the seven sons of King Edward III as "…"seven vials of his sacred blood" (12). She reveals the extent of her loneliness and grief when she invites her other surviving brother-in-law, the Duke of York, to visit her home, but then hastily revokes her invitation: "Alack! and what shall good old York there see/ But empty lodgings and unfurnished walls,/ Unpeopled offices, untrodden stones,/ And what hear there for welcome but my groans?" (67-70).

Act I, Scene 3

New Characters:

Lord Marshal: *a high official at the court of Richard II*

Duke of Aumerle: *son of Edmund, Duke of York, cousin to Richard II and Bolingbroke and nephew to John of Gaunt*

Sir John Bushy: *a courtier and favorite of the King*

Sir William Bagot: *another courtier and royal favorite*

Sir Henry Green: *a third courtier favored by King Richard*

Summary

Scene 3 takes place at the tilting field in Coventry. The Duke of Aumerle tells the Lord Marshal that Bolingbroke and Mowbray are armed and ready for their joust; they await the King's arrival. Trumpets sound, and the King enters with his entourage, which includes John of Gaunt, Bushy, Bagot, Green, and attendants. After the King is seated, Mowbray enters in armor, accompanied by a Herald.

King Richard asks the Marshal to inquire of Mowbray his name and his cause. The Marshal does so, and Mowbray announces that he means, in defending himself, to prove Bolingbroke "…A traitor to my God, my king, and me" (24). The trumpets sound, and Bolingbroke enters, also in armor. Richard asks the Lord Marshall to formally ask the second combatant's name and "why he cometh hither/ Thus plated in habiliments of war" (27-28). Bolingbroke announces his name and cause: "Harry of Hereford, Lancaster and

Derby/ Am I, who ready here do stand in arms/ To prove by God's grace, and my body's valor/ ...That [Mowbray] is a traitor, foul and dangerous" (35-39).

Bolingbroke asks for the privilege of kissing the King's hand and bowing before his sovereign. Richard descends from his throne and embraces him, commenting: "Cousin of Hereford, as the cause is right,/ So be thy fortune in this royal fight." (55-56) He tells Bolingbroke that if he is killed he will lament the loss of a kinsman, but will not avenge his death. Bolingbroke tells the King he is confident he will win. He takes leave of the King and his cousin, the Duke of Aumerle. His father, John of Gaunt, bestows a blessing upon him.

Mowbray then asserts his loyalty to the King and claims that he, too, looks forward to the combat. Richard praises him for his virtue and valor and commands the joust to begin. The Marshal orders lances distributed to the combatants, and the Heralds again announce the names of the adversaries and their causes. A flourish of trumpets sounds, and Bolingbroke and Mowbray prepare to do battle.

An instant later, however, the King throws his staff of office down and orders the combat to a halt. He commands the adversaries to set aside their helmets and spears and return to their chairs. A long flourish of trumpets sounds; the King confers with his council and then bids the adversaries to draw near. He proclaims that rather than seeing one of his countrymen slaughtered, as in a civil war, he has decided to banish both combatants from England. He sentences Bolingbroke to ten years of exile, a sentence Bolingbroke accepts gracefully. Mowbray's penalty is harsher; he is banished from England for life. Mowbray is saddened by his sentence, having anticipated a "dearer merit" from his sovereign, but King Richard is unmoved by his grief and disappointment.

Mowbray turns to go, but Richard calls him back again. He orders Mowbray and Bolingbroke to lay their hands upon his sword and to swear an oath never to "embrace each other's love in banishment" or "by advisèd purpose meet/ To plot, contrive, or complot any ill/ 'Gainst us, our state, our subjects, or our land" (184; 188-190). Mowbray and Bolingbroke swear to uphold his command. Bolingbroke then asks Mowbray to confess his treason

before he journeys into exile. However, Mowbray proclaims his innocence; he tells Bolingbroke: "But what thou art, God, thou, and I, do know/ And all too soon, I fear, the King shall rue" (203-204). He bids the King farewell and exits.

Richard, seeing Gaunt's sorrow at the imminent banishment of his son, promptly reduces Bolingbroke's sentence to six years. Gaunt thanks the King, yet he comments that he does not expect to live long enough to see his son's return. Richard assures his uncle that he has many years to live. However, Gaunt replies wistfully; although duty compels him to respect his sovereign's wishes, not even the King can prolong his life. Richard wonders why Gaunt, when asked for his advice on the matter, did not argue on his son's behalf. Gaunt answers that the King has asked him to speak as an impartial judge and not like a father. He laments the harshness of the royal mandate, but Richard reiterates that Bolingbroke's banishment will be for six years and exits with his courtiers and attendants.

After the King is gone, the Duke of Aumerle bids his banished cousin farewell, and the Lord Marshal pledges to accompany Bolingbroke as far as the coast, where he will board a ship bound for France. Bolingbroke expresses sorrow at his sentence and his father attempts to comfort him: "Call it a travel that thou tak'st for pleasure./ ...Think not the King did banish thee,/ But thou the King." (261; 278-279) Yet Bolingbroke remains saddened by his impending exile, and he prepares reluctantly to leave his beloved native land.

Analysis

Again we are greeted by a formal, public scene, replete with colorful pageantry. As the scene commences, the conflicts introduced in Scene 1 are now to be resolved by the Medieval code of gentlemanly combat. Mowbray and Bolingbroke are announced ceremoniously by the Lord Marshal and their Heralds. They solemnly defend their causes and prepare to do battle. Throughout, Mowbray maintains a posture of quiet confidence, in contrast to Bolingbroke's more emotional response to the proceedings. Here, the adversaries echo their exchanges in Scene 1. Yet we now know that King Richard was responsible for Gloucester's death; Mowbray, in all likelihood, feels that his sovereign will protect him, for he has acted at the King's bidding.

Critics are divided as to Richard's motivations in halting the combat at the climactic moment; some commentators feel he has planned this all along, while others are of the opinion that it is a spur-of-the-moment decision. In either case, his reason for halting the combat seems sound: he proclaims that he has done so "That our kingdom's earth should not be soiled/ With that dear blood which it hath fosterèd" (125-126). Yet here, he makes another veiled allusion to his true feelings for Bolingbroke when he refers to "...sky-aspiring and ambitious thoughts" (130). Note, also, that the King pronounces sentence on the loyal Mowbray with "some unwillingness," and that Mowbray had anticipated a "dearer merit." He is genuinely upset when the King repays his service by banishing him for life, but Richard doubtless realized that it was politically expedient to disassociate himself from a man who can connect him to Gloucester's murder.

Bolingbroke's exile, too, is politically expedient, for, like Gaunt, he is aware of the King's role in Gloucester's death. However, Richard is aware that Gaunt respects his authority; he can well afford a noble gesture toward his son. Here, he plays his kingly role with reasonable efficiency. Yet there is shallow flippancy in his declaration that he has "plucked four away" in reducing Bolingbroke's sentence. Bolingbroke's response eloquently reveals the extent of the King's power: "How long a time lies in one little word" (212). We are also given an indication of the King's character in his condescending response to Gaunt's lament that he expects to die before his son's return: "Why! uncle, thou hast many years to live" (224).

This scene contains a number of examples of dramatic irony. Richard, before the combat, descends from his throne to embrace Bolingbroke, a hypocritical gesture, given what we now know about his complicity in the Duke of Gloucester's murder. When they meet next, he will again descend, but this time from the walls of Flint Castle to surrender his kingdom. When Bolingbroke pledges, at Richard's request, that he will not plot with Mowbray against the crown, it is a pledge he will indeed fulfill. Yet he will, in fact, return with others to lead a rebellion against his sovereign. And Mowbray's assertion that Bolingbroke will one day give the King cause for regret will prove prophetic.

The tender parting between Gaunt and his son at the end of this scene recalls the more personal exchange between Gaunt and the widowed Duchess of Gloucester in Scene 2. Here, what has been a public occasion becomes a private one. We see the loving relationship of father and son and again feel their sorrow at Bolingbroke's impending exile. Bolingbroke's final speech reveals his patriotic fervor and his love of his native land. This speech foreshadows his father's eloquent patriotism in Act II, Scene 1 and his own ultimate return to England.

Act I, Scene 4

Summary

At the court, the King meets with Bagot, Green, and the Duke of Aumerle. Richard, testing Aumerle's loyalty, asks his cousin how far he escorted the banished Bolingbroke "...and what store of parting tears were shed" (5). Aumerle tells the King he pretended to be sad at Bolingbroke's departure, but in truth he was glad to see him go. Richard comments that he and his courtiers have observed that Bolingbroke was ambitious and sought favor with the common people. He worries that the populace might consider Bolingbroke a potential successor to his throne.

"Well, he is gone," Green comments, and he adds that the King must now turn to more pressing matters: a rebellion in Ireland. Richard proclaims, "We will ourself in person to this war" (42). He is aware, however, that the royal treasury is depleted as a result of his lavish expenditures on his court, leaving limited funds for a military campaign. Thus, he proposes to lease royal lands and demand money from his wealthy subjects to finance his expedition. Bushy enters with the news that Old John of Gaunt is gravely ill and has asked the King to visit him. Richard replies callously, "Now put it, God, in the physician's mind/ To help him to his grave immediately!" The money from Gaunt's estate, he comments, "shall make coats/ To deck our soldiers for these Irish wars" (59-62). He prepares to journey to Gaunt's bedside with his courtiers, yet he hopes they will arrive too late and that Gaunt will already be dead.

Analysis

Richard is now at ease with his trusted courtiers. He abandons the formality of his public role and engages in private conversation with his favorites. Here, he relinquishes his impartial public persona and reveals his true feelings about the cousin he had hypocritically embraced in Scene 3. We learn through Richard that Bolingbroke—referred to sarcastically as "high Hereford"—has attempted to curry favor with the common people, and that he has lofty political ambitions. Bolingbroke, Richard remarks, has behaved "As were our England in reversion his/ And he our subjects' next degree in hope" (35-36). Richard speaks of his cousin's "courtship to the common people" with haughty disdain; unlike Bolingbroke, he apparently has little concern with his popularity among the slaves and poor craftsmen of his kingdom.

Later in this scene, Richard reveals new and startling dimensions of his capriciousness. Callous and money hungry, he solves his problems irresponsibly, on the spur of the moment. To put down the Irish rebellion, he resolves to mortgage the future revenues on his royal lands for immediate cash and authorizes blank checks to be written in the names of his subjects, which his agents will then fill in with whatever funds the crown might need. He also expresses the hope that his uncle, John of Gaunt—a respected elder statesman who is loyal to the crown—will die so that he might seize his revenues for use in his Irish campaign. His decision is doubtless based in part upon the hostility he feels toward Bolingbroke, but he fails to recognize the political danger of his plan, given Bolingbroke's popularity and his rebellious nature.

The Duke of Aumerle, who is cousin to the King and to Bolingbroke, reveals that his loyalties lie firmly with Richard. He shed no tears at Bolingbroke's departure, and there is blunt derision in his report of Bolingbroke's leavetaking. Bushy, Bagot, and Green, flattering courtiers all, also side firmly with their sovereign. They echo Richard's hope that Gaunt will die with a gleeful, cold-hearted "Amen."

Study Questions

1. What accusations does Henry Bolingbroke, Duke of Hereford, bring against Thomas Mowbray, Duke of Norfolk?

2. How does King Richard decide to settle the conflict between Bolingbroke and Mowbray?

3. Who does John of Gaunt blame for the Duke of Gloucester's murder?

4. Why does the Duchess of Gloucester revoke her invitation for her brother-in-law, the Duke of York, to visit her?

5. What signal does the King give to halt the combat between Bolingbroke and Mowbray before it begins?

6. What penalties does King Richard initially impose on Bolingbroke and Mowbray?

7. What oath does King Richard make Bolingbroke and Mowbray swear upon his sword?

8. Why does King Richard change the sentence he imposes on Bolingbroke, and what are the terms of his new sentence?

9. How do we know that Bolingbroke is popular among the common people?

10. What is King Richard's response when he learns that John of Gaunt is seriously ill?

Answers

1. Bolingbroke accuses Mowbray of misappropriating funds intended for the King's military forces in France. He also accuses Mowbray of plotting the Duke of Gloucester's murder.

2. King Richard, after failing in his attempts to arbitrate the conflict between Bolingbroke and Mowbray, decrees that they will meet in man to man combat "At Coventry upon Saint Lambert's Day."

3. Gaunt tells his sister-in-law that King Richard was responsible for her husband's murder.

4. The Duchess of Gloucester rescinds her invitation to the Duke of York when she realizes that sorrow will make her a poor hostess.

5. The King throws down his warder (a short staff of office) to halt the combat between Bolingbroke and Mowbray.

6. King Richard banishes Bolingbroke for ten years. He banishes Mowbray for life.

7. The King makes Bolingbroke and Mowbray swear that they will not "embrace each other's love in banishment,/ Nor never look upon each other's face,/ Nor never write, regreet, nor reconcile/ This louring tempest of your home-bred hate." He also makes them pledge never to meet purposefully "To plot, contrive, or complot any ill/ 'Gainst us, our state, our subjects, or our land."

8. King Richard changes Bolingbroke's sentence when he sees that Bolingbroke's father, John of Gaunt, looks sad at the thought of his son's exile. He reduces Bolingbroke's banishment to six years.

9. The King remarks that he and his courtiers have observed Bolingbroke courting the common people's favor: "How he did seem to dive into their hearts/ With humble and familiar courtesy/ ...Wooing poor craftsmen with the craft of smiles."

10. King Richard rejoices when he learns that John of Gaunt is ill. He expresses the hope that Gaunt will die so he can seize his money and lands to help finance his military campaign in Ireland.

Suggested Essay Topics

1. In Act I, Shakespeare alternates public and private scenes. Discuss the behavior of the principal characters in each of these scenes and the ways in which their behavior reflects the nature of their large or small audience.

2. Discuss the positive and negative aspects of King Richard's character revealed in Act I.

3. Examine the ways in which Shakespeare reveals Gaunt's loyalty to the crown and his son's rebellious nature.

4. Explore Shakespeare's frequent use of blood imagery in the first act.

SECTION THREE

Act II

Act II, Scene 1

New Characters:

Edmund, Duke of York: *uncle to Richard II and Bolingbroke and father of the Duke of Aumerle; brother to John of Gaunt*

Earl of Northumberland: *a nobleman who sides with Henry Bolingbroke when he learns that Bolingbroke is returning from his banishment*

Lord Willoughby: *a nobleman loyal to the Earl of Northumberland*

Lord Ross: *another nobleman loyal to the Earl of Northumberland*

Queen Isabel: *second wife to Richard II*

Summary

At Ely House in London, we encounter the dying John of Gaunt. Also present are Edmund, Duke of York (Gaunt's brother), the Earl of Northumberland, and their attendants. Gaunt asks his brother whether the King will come; he hopes to spend his final moments offering "…wholesome counsel to his unstaid youth" (2). The Duke of York tells Gaunt that the King is unlikely to listen to his advice: "All in vain comes counsel to his ear." But Gaunt assures his brother that "the tongues of dying men/ Enforce attention" (4-6). York responds that King Richard listens only to the flattery of his courtiers, to the "lascivious metres" of popular songs and poetry, and to

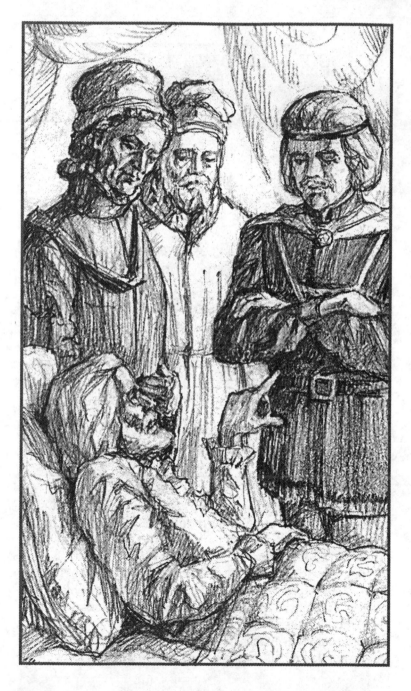

news of the latest fashions from Italy; he is more interested in frivolity than in wise counsel.

Gaunt speaks patriotically and at length about his beloved England and the proud tradition of its kings. He expresses his shame that under the reign of King Richard the nation seems destined for ruin; much of the royal land has now been leased out to raise funds for the crown, and the kingdom "that was wont to conquer others/ Hath made a shameful conquest of itself" (65-66).

King Richard enters with Queen Isabel, Aumerle, Bushy, Green, Bagot, Lord Ross, and Lord Willoughby. The Duke of York urges his brother to "deal mildly with his youth,/ For young hot colts being raged do rage the more" (69-70). The King and Queen inquire politely as to Gaunt's health, and Gaunt puns that his name is appropriate, for in his final illness he is gaunt, indeed. Yet he is also gaunt with sorrow at his son's banishment and at the King's mismanagement of his realm. He comments that while he is physically ill, Richard is "in reputation sick," and has surrounded himself with "a thousand flatterers." He then remarks to the King that had Richard's grandfather "with a prophet's eye/ Seen how his son's son should destroy his sons,/ From forth thy reach he would have laid thy shame/ Deposing thee before thou wert possessed,/ Which art possessed now to depose thyself" (104-108). He tells Richard bluntly, "Landlord of England art thou now, not king."

Richard angrily interrupts his dying uncle's criticism, calling him a "lunatic, lean-witted fool." If Gaunt were not his uncle, he remarks, he would have him beheaded. However, Gaunt, with equal anger, openly chastises the King for ordering the Duke of Gloucester's murder. He tells the King, "These words hereafter thy tormentors be," and calls for his attendants to "Convey me to my bed, then to my grave" (137-138). The attendants bear him away, escorted by Northumberland.

King Richard petulantly looks forward to Gaunt's death, but his uncle, the Duke of York, attempts to smooth things over: "Impute his words/ To wayward sickliness and age in him:/ He loves you, on my life, and holds you dear/ As Harry, Duke of Hereford, were he here" (141-144). The Earl of Northumberland enters soon afterward with the news that Gaunt is dead. King Richard receives

the announcement callously, and he immediately turns his attention to the Irish wars. To finance his war effort, he seizes Gaunt's
"plate, coin, revenues, and movables" for the crown.

The Duke of York, grief stricken at his brother's death, is furious that Richard has confiscated the property that should right-
fully be inherited by Gaunt's son, the banished Henry Bolingbroke.
He warns Richard that although he is king "by fair sequence and
succession," he is challenging the entire system that brought him
the crown if he wrongfully seizes Bolingbroke's inheritance. He also
warns the King that he will "pluck a thousand dangers" on his head
and "lose a thousand well-disposèd hearts" if he carries through
on his plan. However, Richard refuses to heed his uncle's warning
and reiterates his intention to seize Gaunt's estate. York bids his
nephew farewell; he tells the King that he cannot predict the consequences of his actions. After York leaves, Richard announces his
plan to sail for Ireland in two days. He appoints York Lord Governor in his absence and exits with the Queen and his courtiers.
Northumberland, Willoughby, and Ross remain.

Northumberland remarks tersely on the injustice of the situation they have witnessed, and he adds that "The King is not himself, but basely led/ By flatterers" (241-242). Ross notes that the
King has levied excessive taxes on the common people and fined
the nobles, and in doing so has "quite lost their hearts." All agree
that the situation in England is grim; they are distressed by
Richard's high-handed policies and feel that he is unfit to be king.
Northumberland then reveals a startling piece of news: he has
learned that Bolingbroke, along with a number of sympathetic
noblemen and three thousand soldiers, has left his exile in France
and set sail for England. Their arrival is imminent as they are waiting only for the King to depart for Ireland. Northumberland views
Bolingbroke's arrival as an opportunity for the nobles to "shake off
our slavish yoke" (291). He urges Willoughby and Ross to accompany him when he journeys to meet Bolingbroke, and they swiftly
agree.

Analysis

At the beginning of this scene, John of Gaunt, one of the last
survivors of the old order— Richard's father's generation—desires

only to share his wisdom with the King. Gaunt is aware that Richard has in the past paid little heed to wise counsel, yet he believes that he will pay special attention to his dying words: "My death's sad tale may yet undeaf his ear" (16). The Duke of York is more pragmatic. He believes, correctly, as it turns out, that the luxury-loving King will listen only to his favorites and flatterers. Gaunt's wisdom here is a sharp contrast to Richard's shallow ridicule in the previous scene; he prophesies that Richard's "rash fierce blaze of riot cannot last."

Gaunt's description of England is one of the most famed passages in Shakespeare. In this stirring speech, he makes clear his love of his native land: "This royal throne of kings, this scept'red isle / This earth of majesty, this seat of Mars, / This other Eden, demi-paradise, / . . . This blessed plot, this earth, this realm, this England" (40-42; 50). Here, he echoes his son's patriotism at the end of Act I, Scene 3 and comments eloquently on England's virtues and the noble heritage of its monarchy. When he remarks bitterly that England has "made a shameful conquest of itself," he is referring directly to King Richard's mismanagement of the realm. His idealized depiction of England is in sharp contrast to actual conditions resulting from Richard's misrule.

The King's polite greeting to his dying uncle is rife with hypocrisy, given what we have seen of his behavior in the previous scene. After Richard arrives, Gaunt puns ironically on his name: he is "gaunt as a grave." His imminent death gives him the courage to tell the King that he has disgraced England by his erratic policies. Note that he invokes Richard's grandfather, the honored warrior-king Edward III, when he comments ruefully that had Edward been able to foresee Richard's misdeeds he would have deposed his grandson before he inherited the crown. Thus, we are given additional justification for the rebellion and deposition that will ultimately ensue.

After the King, outraged by Gaunt's insubordination, angrily interrupts his uncle's reproachful accusations, Gaunt, with equal fury, rebukes Richard for his part in Gloucester's murder. Earlier, Gaunt had commented upon his respect for the institution of the crown, yet here he loses that veneration after Richard's callous response to his criticism.

When news is brought of Gaunt's death, the elderly Duke of York, now the last surviving son of King Edward III, also expresses rage at the King's thoughtless actions: "How long shall I be patient? Ah, how long/ Shall tender duty make me suffer wrong?" (163-164) Like his brother, York is conservative by nature; he, too, has a strong sense of duty to the monarchy. Yet he also possesses a keen sense of right and wrong. His extended reference to Richard's father (171-183) contrasts the virtues of father and son—the righteous warrior-prince and his capricious heir. Although Richard resembles his late father, York remarks pointedly, he seems to have inherited few of his noble qualities. But Richard greets his criticism with the flippancy he revealed in earlier scenes: "Why, uncle, what's the matter?"

York, deeply troubled by his nephew's actions, protests that the banished Bolingbroke is rightful heir to Gaunt's estate. Although by law Bolingbroke could not immediately claim his father's property if Gaunt died while he was in exile, Richard had granted him "letters patent" which entitled him to do so when he returned after his term of banishment. Yet Richard now revokes the letters patent, disinheriting Bolingbroke entirely. Significantly, York reminds Richard that he is king by the same laws of inheritance that he has ignored in seizing Bolingbroke's patrimony: "For how art thou a king/ But by fair sequence and succession?" (198-199). He warns Richard that if he seizes Gaunt's property he will be upsetting the entire social order. Yet the King, headstrong, morally weak, and confident of his absolute power, ignores his uncle's warning and reiterates his plan to seize Gaunt's estate, thus providing ample motive for Bolingbroke's subsequent return.

After the King and his courtiers have exited, Northumberland, Willoughby, and Ross, prominent noblemen from the north who have witnessed Richard's capricious behavior toward his uncles and the seizure of Gaunt's estate, offer a further list of grievances against the King. Richard has been influenced adversely by his flattering courtiers; reproach and dissolution hang over him. Not only has Bolingbroke been "gelded of his patrimony"; Richard has taxed the common people excessively and levied fines against the nobles. In doing so, he has lost the support of both groups. Here, we see the seeds of rebellion stirring in the discontent of the northern lords.

Northumberland is unambiguous in his meaning when he suggests that they "Redeem from broking pawn the blemished crown,/ Wipe off the dust that hides our sceptre's gilt,/ And make high majesty look like itself" (293-295).

We now know that Bolingbroke will soon return to England with his aristocratic supporters and an army, although he has pragmatically delayed his landing until the King departs for Ireland. Northumberland, a canny politician, senses that the mood of Willoughby and Ross matches his own and urges them to ally with Bolingbroke's cause. Clearly, Bolingbroke will have further support when he lands.

Act II, Scene 2

Summary

At Windsor Castle, we encounter the Queen, along with Bushy and Bagot. Bushy attempts to comfort the Queen, who is saddened by King Richard's departure for Ireland. The Queen, at her parting from her husband, had agreed to be cheerful for Richard's sake, yet she foresees that "Some unborn sorrow ripe in Fortune's womb/ Is coming towards me" (10-11). Bushy assures her that she is being unduly pessimistic. A moment later, however, Green enters and expresses the hope that the King and his army have not yet departed, for Bolingbroke and his forces have landed at Ravenspurgh, on the northern coast. The Queen is shocked at this news, and she is further alarmed when she learns that the Earl of Northumberland and other noblemen have sided with Bolingbroke's cause.

The Duke of York, now Lord Protector in Richard's absence, enters and announces that he is ill-equipped to deal with a military crisis. A Servingman enters immediately afterward and tells York that his son, the Duke of Aumerle, is nowhere to be found; York fears that his son has allied with Bolingbroke. York then attempts to send the Servingman to his sister-in-law, the Duchess of Gloucester; he hopes to borrow money to suppress Bolingbroke's rebellion. But the Servingman announces further misfortune: the Duchess is dead. The Duke laments that "a tide of woes/ Comes rushing on this woeful land at once," and he confesses, "I know

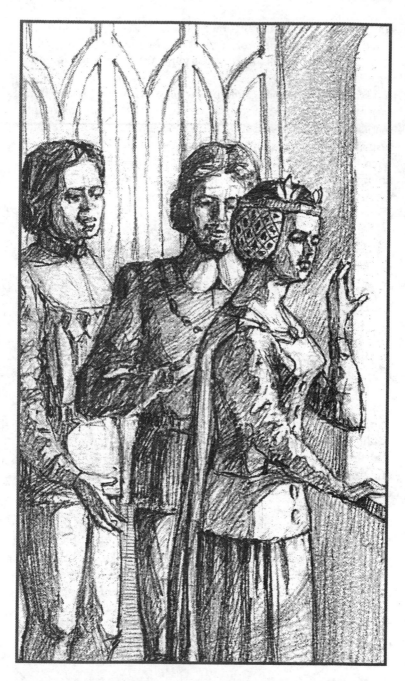

not what to do" (98-100). Richard and Bolingbroke are both his nephews; he has sworn to defend the kingdom, yet he knows that Bolingbroke has been wronged. He resolves to muster an army to confront the rebel forces and exits with the Queen.

After he is gone, Bushy admits candidly that it will be impossible for the crown to raise an army comparable to Bolingbroke's rebel forces; the winds in the Irish channel will assist a ship bringing the news to the King, but will delay Richard's return to England with his soldiers. He acknowledges that the King has fallen out of favor with the common people: "their love/ Lies in their purses, and whoso empties them/ By so much fills their hearts with deadly hate"(128-130). Bagot adds that he, Bushy, and Green, as royal favorites, are now in grave danger. Bushy and Green resolve to seek refuge at Bristow Castle with the Earl of Wiltshire, while Bagot decides to journey to Ireland to join the King's army. "We three here part that ne'er shall meet again," Bagot comments grimly (142). Green, equally pessimistic, predicts that York's efforts to defend the crown are destined to fail: "Alas, poor Duke, the task he undertakes/ Is numb'ring sands, and drinking oceans dry" (144-145).

Analysis

In this scene, Queen Isabel speaks at length for the first time. Although present in the previous scene, she had only a single line of greeting to the dying Gaunt. Historically, Richard's Queen was only ten years old at the time of his Irish campaign. Richard's first wife had died four years earlier, and he subsequently made an arranged marriage with the daughter of the King of France. Shakespeare chose to take liberties with history, however, and made the Queen a young woman. His dramatic license is understandable, both in this scene and in scenes to come, for Queen Isabel will serve a vital dramatic function in the play: Richard's growing misfortunes will be underscored by her concern for her husband.

The Queen, devoted to her "sweet Richard," is genuinely grieved at his absence. We now see the King from a different vantage point. Although Richard has been depicted as callous and irresponsible in earlier scenes, he is presented here in a more sympathetic light: as one who is loved and missed.

The Queen's premonition of an unknown sorrow to come

is soon fulfilled by the grim tidings brought by Green, the Servingman, and York. We are greeted by a sense of gathering doom as one woe follows another: Bolingbroke has landed and mounted a rebellion, the Duchess of Gloucester is dead, and the royal forces are unprepared to deal with an armed insurrection.

Although the Duke of York reaffirms his loyalty to the institution of the crown, it is clear that his emotions are divided; he is also aware of the unjustness of Richard's decree that stripped Bolingbroke of his inheritance. Even so, he resolves to attend to his duty as protector of the realm in Richard's absence, although he is pragmatic about his unpreparedness to suppress Bolingbroke's insurrection. Bushy, Bagot, and Green, favorites of the King, are also pragmatic; they realize that their executions are likely if Bolingbroke prevails. Note that only Bagot resolves to join the King's forces, Bushy and Green reveal their cowardice when they decide to seek refuge rather than fight for their sovereign.

Act II, Scenes 3 and 4

New Characters:

Harry Percy: *son of the Earl of Northumberland*

Earl of Berkeley: *a nobleman and ally of King Richard*

Welsh Captain: *commander of the Welsh soldiers in the service of King Richard*

Earl of Salisbury: *a nobleman loyal to King Richard; commander of the King's army*

Summary

In the Gloucestershire countryside, the banished Bolingbroke and his soldiers have now united with the Earl of Northumberland and his followers. Bolingbroke plans to march toward Berkeley and a meeting with the crown forces led by the Duke of York. Harry Percy, the Earl of Northumberland's son, enters; he brings the news that the Earl of Worcester, formerly steward of the royal household, has broken his staff of office and allied with Bolingbroke. Anticipating a battle, he has sent Percy to make an inspection of the size

of the Duke of York's army. Northumberland introduces his son to
Bolingbroke. Percy pledges his services to Bolingbroke's cause. Lord
Ross and Lord Willoughby enter and greet Bolingbroke with re-
spectful praise.

The Earl of Berkeley arrives on the scene with a message from
the Duke of York. Bolingbroke assures him that his only intention
is to claim his title as Duke of Lancaster and his inherited lands.
The Duke of York arrives immediately afterward. Bolingbroke
kneels at his feet and greets him as "my noble uncle," but York tells
his nephew, "Show me thy humble heart, and not thy knee,/ Whose
duty is deceivable and false" (83-84). He calls Bolingbroke a traitor
and chastises him for returning from banishment to rebel against
his sovereign while the King is away in Ireland.

Bolingbroke again asserts that he is interested only in claim-
ing the dukedom and lands he was bequeathed upon his father's
death: "I was banished Hereford/ But as I come, I come for
Lancaster" (112-113). York admits that King Richard is in the wrong;
he tells Bolingbroke he has "labored all I could to do him right"
(141). However, he reprimands Bolingbroke for leading an armed
rebellion against his sovereign. Northumberland reiterates that
Bolingbroke means only to claim his inheritance, and he pledges
his support.

York confesses that he sees "the issue of these arms" and he
acknowledges that his army is too weak to do battle with
Bolingbroke's forces. If it were possible, he proclaims, he would
make Bolingbroke and his soldiers "stoop/ Unto the sovereign
mercy of the King" (155-156). Since he cannot do so, he promises
that he will remain neutral in the conflict. He offers Bolingbroke
and his allies lodging for the night. Bolingbroke accepts; he adds
that he would like York to accompany him to Bristow Castle, where
Bushy, Bagot, and their accomplices—"the caterpillars of the commonwealth,/ Which I have sworn to weed and pluck away"—have
taken refuge (165-166). York responds that he may decide to accompany Bolingbroke, but for the moment he will defer his decision, since he is "loath to break our country's laws." He adds that
"Things past redress are now with me past care" (168; 170).

In Scene 4, set in Wales, the Earl of Salisbury, commander of
Richard's armies in England, meets with a Welsh Captain. The

Captain announces that his soldiers are restless after waiting ten days for "tidings from the King" to arrive. He therefore plans to disperse his troops. Salisbury asks the Captain to wait another day, adding, "The King reposeth all his confidence in thee." But the Captain responds, "'Tis thought the King is dead: we will not stay" (6-7). He remarks that a number of omens—withered trees, meteor showers, a red moon—have seemingly prophesied "the death or fall of kings" (15). He tells Salisbury that many of his countrymen have already deserted, thinking Richard has been killed in Ireland. The Captain exits; Salisbury laments that he anticipates King Richard's glory will "like a shooting star/ Fall to the base earth from the firmament." In the future, he foresees only "storms to come, woe and unrest" (19-20; 22).

Analysis

In Scene 3, we learn that more nobles have joined Bolingbroke's cause, particularly the Earl of Worcester. Harry Percy, although a minor character in this play, will later be featured prominently in Shakespeare's *Henry IV, Part 1*. Here, he represents the idealism of Bolingbroke's followers.

Bolingbroke, in turn, is depicted as a born leader who has moved steadily and purposefully toward his goal. Note that the Earl of Northumberland, Percy's father, had earlier railed against Richard's flattering courtiers (II, i, 241-242), yet here, ironically, he addresses Bolingbroke with elaborate and deferential praise.

Bolingbroke twice asserts that his only wish is to claim his rightful title as Duke of Lancaster and the lands he inherited from his late father. Critics differ in their opinions as to whether Bolingbroke returned to England with the aim of seizing the crown, or whether circumstances directed his course after his landing. Note, however, that he confesses that one of his aims is to "weed and pluck away" enemies of the state—a privilege granted only to the monarch.

Bolingbroke's passion in the first act has now been supplanted by a more dignified, stalwart manner, a confidence born of strength which he will retain in subsequent scenes. We are reminded frequently in this scene that Bolingbroke has returned to England with a legitimate grievance. Yet here, too, we are greeted by a number of reminders that Richard, although capricious, is the rightful sovereign. The Duke of York, although sympathetic to Bolingbroke's claim to his inheritance, tells Bolingbroke in no uncertain terms that he is committing "gross rebellion and detested treason" against his "annointed King."

Bolingbroke is deferential when responding to his uncle's charges, yet at the same time he is subtly wooing him to his cause; he remarks that "You are my father, for methinks in you/ I see old Gaunt alive" (116-117). He also argues logically that in seizing Gaunt's estate, Richard has struck a blow against the entire system of aristocratic inheritance—the same system which enabled Richard to inherit the crown. Here, he echoes York's similar pronouncement in Act II, Scene 1. Although York professes neutrality, he indicates his true feelings when he offers Bolingbroke hospitality in his castle.

In Scene 4, the brief exchange between the Earl of Salisbury and the Welsh Captain provides a further indication of Richard's growing misfortunes. The omens related by the Welsh Captain are of a world in disorder, of nature run amok; catastrophe seems imminent. Throughout the play, the sun will serve as an emblem of Richard's kingship, yet here the sun "sets weeping," and Richard is described by Salisbury as a shooting star plummeting rapidly from the heavens.

Study Questions

1. Why does John of Gaunt hope that King Richard will visit him on his deathbed?

2. What possessions does King Richard seize after Gaunt dies?

3. Who does King Richard appoint Lord Governor of England in his absence?

4. What news does the Earl of Northumberland share with Lord Willoughby and Lord Ross?

5. Why has Bolingbroke delayed his arrival in England?

6. What reasons does the Queen give to explain her sadness?

7. What information does Sir Henry Green deliver to the Queen?

8. Whose death does the Servingman report to the Duke of York?

9. What does the Duke of York tell Bolingbroke his official position will be in Bolingbroke's conflict with King Richard?

10. What omens have made the Welsh Captain believe that King Richard is dead?

Answers

1. John of Gaunt hopes that King Richard will visit him on his deathbed so that he might "breathe my last/ In wholesome counsel" to the King. Although Richard has, in the past, paid little heed to his advice, Gaunt believes that he will pay attention to the words of a dying man.

2. After Gaunt dies, King Richard seizes his "plate, his goods, his money, and his lands."

3. King Richard appoints his uncle, the Duke of York, as Lord Governor of England.

4. The Earl of Northumberland tells Willoughby and Ross that Bolingbroke, along with a number of noblemen loyal to his cause and an army of three thousand men, has set sail from France. He and his supporters will soon arrive in England.

5. Bolingbroke is waiting for the King and his army to depart for Ireland so they will not be able to offer resistance when he lands.

6. The Queen is sad because the King has departed for Ireland. She is also sad because she foresees that "Some unborn sorrow in Fortune's womb is coming towards me."

7. Green brings the news that Henry Bolingbroke, armed for combat, has landed safely at Ravenspurgh, on the northern coast. He also tells the Queen that the Earl of Northumberland, his son Harry Percy, and a number of other noblemen have allied with Bolingbroke's cause.

8. The Servingman tells York that his sister-in-law, the Duchess of Gloucester, is dead.

9. York tells Bolingbroke that he plans to be neutral in the conflict.

10. The Welsh Captain reports that "The bay trees in our country are all withered,/ And meteors fright the fixèd stars of heaven,/ The pale-faced moon looks bloody on the earth,/ And lean-looked prophets whisper fearful change." These signs, he remarks, "foretell the death or fall of kings." Moreover, his countrymen believe that the King is dead.

Suggested Essay Topics

1. Examine the validity of the charges brought against the King by the dying John of Gaunt.

2. Discuss the ways in which Shakespeare reveals that Bolingbroke, the nobles, and the common people have just cause to be angry with Richard's policies as sovereign.

3. Explore the reasons why the Duke of York is torn between the causes of his nephews, King Richard and Henry Bolingbroke.

4. Discuss the ways in which the events of the second act foreshadow King Richard's downfall.

Act III

Act III, Scene 1

Summary

This scene is set in Bristol, in front of the castle. Bolingbroke, York, and Northumberland enter along with other Lords and Soldiers; they have taken Bushy and Green as prisoners. Bolingbroke proclaims that Bushy and Green will soon be executed. He accuses them of having misled the King. Furthermore, they have brought divisions between the King and Queen, and between the King and Bolingbroke. He holds them personally responsible for his banishment and the subsequent looting of his father's estate and hands them over for execution. Bushy and Green respond defiantly and welcome their fate, and Northumberland leads them off to the chopping block. Bolingbroke comments to the Duke of York that he wishes the Queen, residing at York's palace in London, to be treated fairly; he sends her his "kind commends." He then orders his army away to do battle with the Welsh soldiers allied with King Richard.

Analysis

Here, we see further misfortune for King Richard in the capture and subsequent executions of Bushy and Green, two of the King's favorites. When Bolingbroke charges Richard's courtiers with having "misled a prince, a royal king," (8) he is reiterating the charge made by his father on his deathbed. He blames them specifically for his estrangement from the King, his banishment, and

the pillaging of his inherited lands and manor house. Although there is some validity to his accusations, he is also making a propaganda speech for the benefit of his followers. It is uncertain what Bolingbroke means by his reference to Bushy and Green making "a divorce" between the King and Queen, although Holinshed's *Chronicles*, Shakespeare's principal source for this play, refers to the King's adultery. Shakespeare may also be implying that a homosexual relationship among the King and his courtiers was the cause of Richard's estrangement from his Queen. This theme was present in Marlowe's *Edward II*, another Elizabethan drama about an ill-fated English monarch, and one that may have influenced Shakespeare when he was writing this play. Ironically, Bushy, in his exchange with the Queen in Act II, Scene 2, was concerned primarily with comforting her grief at Richard's absence. It is also difficult to reconcile this accusation with what we learn of the relationship between the King and Queen elsewhere in the play.

Bolingbroke, despite his public statements that he seeks only his rightful inheritance, is clearly acting in a kingly manner when he orders the beheadings of Richard's courtiers. In doing so, he reveals the true extent of his ambitions. He shows compassion, however, when he commands that the Queen is to be treated with kindness. This alternation of harshness and mercy will typify his behavior in scenes to come.

Act III, Scene 2

New Characters:

Bishop of Carlisle: *a clergyman loyal to King Richard*

Sir Stephen Scroop: *a soldier and ally of the King*

Summary

Scene 2 takes place on the Welsh coast, near Barkloughly Castle. With a flourish of trumpets and drums, the King, the Duke of Aumerle, and the Bishop of Carlisle enter, along with Soldiers and Attendants. King Richard, after a rough crossing of the Irish Sea, expresses joy at arriving once again in his kingdom. He weeps and caresses his native soil "...as a long-parted mother with her

child" (8). He is aware of Bolingbroke's insurrection, and he urges the land itself to rise up against "foul rebellion's arms." The Bishop of Carlisle assures him that the royal cause is a just one, and that the powers of heaven will ensure that he remains King. Yet he advises Richard not to neglect "the means that heavens yield." The Duke of Aumerle also entreats the King to take practical action: "We are too remiss,/ Whilst Bolingbroke through our security/ Grows strong and great in substance and in power" (33-35). Yet Richard, comparing himself to the sun, proclaims confidently that thieves and murderers flourish when the sun is absent, but they "stand bare and naked, trembling at themselves" when it rises once again in the east (46). Bolingbroke, he comments, will "tremble at his sin" after learning that he has returned to England. He asserts his divine right to govern and proclaims that the powers of heaven will safeguard his throne.

Soon afterward, the Earl of Salisbury enters with distressing news: he tells the King he has returned from Ireland one day too late, and that the twelve thousand Welsh soldiers he had mustered have deserted or defected to Bolingbroke. The King turns pale when he hears these tidings. Aumerle attempts to rally his spirits: "Comfort, my liege, remember who you are." Richard swiftly regains his composure: "I had forgot myself: am I not King?" (82-83). He insists that the Duke of York "hath power enough" to suppress the rebellion.

A moment later, however, Sir Stephen Scroop enters with another message of woe. The King prepares himself for the worst: "Say, is my kingdom lost?" Scroop confirms the King's fears. He tells Richard that Bolingbroke's forces have swept across England, and that the common people—bearded old men, young boys, even the women—have taken up arms for his cause. Richard inquires about the fate of the Earl of Wiltshire and his favored courtiers, Bushy, Bagot, and Green: "I warrant they have made peace with Bolingbroke." "Peace have they made with him indeed, my lord," Scroop replies (127-128). Richard, enraged, calls them "villains, vipers ...Judases," but Scroop tells him to "uncurse their souls" and explains what he meant: Wiltshire, Bushy, and Green have been captured and beheaded. Aumerle asks Scroop the whereabouts of his father, the Duke of York, and the army he is leading, but

Richard interjects woefully, "No matter where—of comfort no man speak./ Let's talk of graves, of worms, and epitaphs/ ...Our lands, our lives, and all are Bolingbroke's" (144-145; 151). Self-consciously anticipating his own martyrdom, he meditates mournfully and philosophically on the death of kings.

The Bishop of Carlisle urges Richard to fight on to the last; his advice that "wise men ne'er sit and wail their woes,/ But presently prevent the ways to wail" stirs Richard from his self pity (178-179). Aumerle assures the King that his father still maintains the royal army. Richard, heartened by their encouragement, resolves to continue the battle against Bolingbroke's insurrection. He asks Scroop the current location of York's forces. But Scroop has more bad news to deliver. He tells the King that York has allied with Bolingbroke, that the northern castles have all been conquered, and that the southern lords have joined Bolingbroke's cause. Richard immediately recognizes the futility of his situation; he resolves to seek refuge at Flint Castle nearby, there to "pine away," and he discharges his remaining soldiers to return to their lands.

Analysis

Richard's joyous declaration of how happy he is "To stand upon my kingdom once again" (5) and his subsequent paean to his native soil are ironic, for we know with what little regard he has held his kingdom. Here, his speech seems a hollow echo of the dying John of Gaunt's patriotic sentiments in Act II, Scene 1. Note that he is not only praising his native soil, but is also urging it to rise up against the invading Bolingbroke. His sentiments, although sincere, are clearly overstated. Even the King realizes the excess of his words when he remarks: "Mock not my senseless conjuration, lords" (24).

Again, we are greeted by the theme of the divine right of kings when the Bishop of Carlisle assures his sovereign that "the power that made you king/ Hath power to keep you king" (27-28). Richard reiterates this thought when he proclaims confidently, "Not all the water in the rough rude sea/ Can wash the balm off from an annointed king;/ The breath of worldly men cannot depose/ The deputy elected by the Lord" (54-57). For every soldier in

Bolingbroke's army, Richard asserts, he, in turn, has an angel in heaven to defend his cause.

Yet Carlisle and Aumerle wisely counsel the King to take practical measures. They tell him diplomatically that the Lord helps those who help themselves, and that soldiers will be more useful than angels in this particular crisis. Richard, however, perversely refuses to believe that any harm can come to a divinely annointed king.

Even so, Richard is visibly shaken when Salisbury enters to announce that his Welsh soldiers have deserted. At first, he is optimistic that York's forces can suppress the rebellion, yet he realizes instantly that Scroop has arrived as the bearer of bad news. Hope turns to despair and his remaining optimism erodes rapidly when Scroop tells him that Bolingbroke has gained the support from the common people as he journeyed across the land. When he believes that his loyal courtiers have deserted to Bolingbroke's cause he continues to allude to his divine right by calling them "Judases." When he learns the truth of the matter—that Bushy, Green, and the Earl of Wiltshire have been executed—we arrive at a major turning point, both in the play and in King Richard's character.

In the extended meditation that follows, Richard reveals a new facet to his complex personality. In defeat, he emerges as an eloquent philosopher and a sensitive, intelligent poet. He begins to take on the dimensions of a tragic hero. His tone is self-pitying as he becomes conscious of the disparity between his role of divine monarch and his all-too-human despair, yet the hopelessness of his situation yields soul-searching poetry. In the first two acts, Richard has been depicted as unjust and capricious, but here he appears in a far more sympathetic light.

In one of the most famed passages in this play, Richard responds to the swift reality of what has occurred by telling those gathered with him: "For God's sake let us sit upon the ground/ And tell sad stories of the death of kings/ ...for within the hollow crown/ That rounds the mortal temples of a king/ Keeps death his court" (155-156; 160-162). Later in this speech, Richard refutes the "divinity" which he had spoken of only moments earlier and poignantly refers to himself as only a man: "You have but mistook me all this while:/ I live with bread like you, feel want,/ Taste grief, need friends—subjected thus,/ How can you say to me, I am a king?" (174-177). Here, for the first time, we see a new and more human dimension to his character. Though he is clearly assuming a role—that of a martyred King—his sorrow is genuine.

We can, of course, see elements of the capriciousness he evinced in the first two acts in his rapidly changing moods throughout this scene—he alternates between exhilaration and despair. His instability and weakness of character are apparent in his indecisive response to Bolingbroke's military threat. Although he has vowed to fight valiantly for his cause, he capitulates without a struggle after Scroop delivers the news that York has allied with the rebels.

When Richard, resigned to his fate, discharges the few soldiers he has left "To ear the land that hath some hope to grow," (212) his generosity seems uncharacteristic of the sovereign we have known earlier. Nevertheless, his concern for his soldiers and his hope that their land might prove fertile is evidently sincere. Prior to this scene, Richard has been offstage for more than four hundred lines; he has been transformed by his voyage to Ireland, and by the series of disasters he encountered after his return. He is now more articulate and self-aware than when he set sail. In defeat he is a pitiable figure, but his poetic eloquence grants him a new stature.

When Richard tells Aumerle, "He does me double wrong/ That wounds me with the flatteries of his tongue," it serves as a reminder that one of the principal charges made earlier against the King was that he listened only to his flattering courtiers. Yet he has no interest in flattery once he realizes the scene has changed "From Richard's night to Bolingbroke's fair day" (215-216; 218).

Act III, Scene 3

Summary

Scene 3 takes place on the northeast coast of Wales, before Flint Castle. Bolingbroke, York, and Northumberland enter along with their soldiers. Bolingbroke has learned that the Welsh army has dispersed, and that the Earl of Salisbury has gone to meet the King. Northumberland tells Bolingbroke that "Richard not far from hence hath hid his head" (6).

Harry Percy delivers the message soon afterward that Flint Castle has refused to yield and is "royally manned" against Bolingbroke's entrance; the King and his few remaining supporters are within. Bolingbroke orders Northumberland to tell the King that he "sends allegience and true faith of heart/ To his most royal person; hither come/ Even at his feet to lay my arms and power,/ Provided that my banishment is repealed,/ And lands restored again be freely granted" (36-40). If King Richard refuses his request, however, he resolves to regain his title and lands by force. Yet he orders his soldiers to march "without the noise of threat'ning drum" as they parade outside the castle in a show of strength, and he hopes for an amicable meeting with the King.

Bolingbroke's trumpets sound a flourish; Richard's trumpets answer. The King appears on the walls of the castle, accompanied by the Bishop of Carlisle, Aumerle, Scroop, and Salisbury. Northumberland approaches the castle and Richard addresses him. He tells him he is "amazed" that an insurrection should be mounted against the lawful monarch, God's annointed. He rebukes Northumberland for not showing proper courtesy to his sovereign and proclaims defiantly: "God omnipotent,/ Is mustering in his clouds on our behalf/ Armies of pestilence, and they shall strike/ Your children yet unborn and unbegot/ That lift your vassal hands against my head/ And threat the glory of my precious crown" (84-89).

Richard commands Northumberland to return to Bolingbroke to inform him that he is a traitor who has come to open "...the purple testament of bleeding war" (93). He warns Northumberland that before the crown that Bolingbroke looks for lives in peace, much English blood will be shed. Northumberland replies diplomatically that the divine right of kings prohibits that the castle should be taken by force. He assures the King that Bolingbroke has come humbly; he has sworn by his ancestors' graves and by his honor as a nobleman that he desires only the restoration of his title and lands. This being granted, he will disband his army and devote himself to "...faithful service of your Majesty" (117).

Richard tells Northumberland that Bolingbroke is welcome, and that his "fair demands" will be met. After Northumberland leaves to convey this message, however, Richard confesses to

Aumerle that he is tempted to "send/ Defiance to the traitor and so die" (128-129). Aumerle counsels the King that it is better to wait until "time lends friends, and friends their helpful swords" (131). Richard, suddenly overcome by sorrow, laments that it is necessary to revoke his royal sentence of banishment and cries out in despair: "O, that I were as great/ As is my grief, or lesser than my name!" (135-136).

Northumberland returns from conferring with Bolingbroke. Before he can deliver his message, however, Richard proclaims: "What must the King do now? Must he submit?/ The King shall do it. Must he be deposed?/ The King shall be contented" (142-144). He mournfully anticipates the life he will lead after giving up his kingdom: the trappings of royalty will be replaced by an austere life of religious contemplation and ultimately, an obscure grave.

Aumerle is reduced to tears by his sovereign's melancholy reflections and Richard attempts to comfort him. Then, abruptly shifting his mood, Richard asks Northumberland sarcastically: "What says King Bolingbroke? Will his Majesty/ Give Richard leave to live till Richard die?" (172-173). Northumberland states that Bolingbroke desires only to speak with the King, and he bids him to come down from the castle walls. "Down, down I come, like glist'ring Phaethon/ ...at traitors' calls," Richard shouts defiantly. He withdraws from the ramparts; Northumberland returns to Bolingbroke and warns him that "sorrow and grief of heart" have made the King speak foolishly, "like a frantic man."

Richard and his attendants enter on the lower level a moment later. Bolingbroke tells his nobles and soldiers, "Stand all apart,/ And show fair duty to his Majesty" (185-186). He kneels deferentially at Richard's feet and tells him, "I come but for mine own." Richard replies, "Your own is yours, and I am yours, and all." (194-195) He comforts his uncle, the Duke of York, who is in tears and then asks Bolingbroke, "Set on towards London, cousin, is it so?" When Bolingbroke responds in the affirmative, Richard replies, with ironic humor: "Then I must not say no" (206-207).

Analysis

This scene is in many ways a reprise of Act I, Scene 3, in which the duel between Bolingbroke and Mowbray was scheduled to take place. Again, we anticipate a battle, but no actual combat occurs. Bolingbroke has assembled an army to meet the King's soldiers, but they never fight. Instead, there is a formal, ceremonious meeting and Richard submits meekly.

Northumberland is openly hopeful that Bolingbroke will assume the throne. Bolingbroke, on the other hand, is more guarded about his ultimate ambitions. Although he realizes that he has triumphed over the royal forces, he still proclaims publicly that his allegience is to the King, and he continues to assert that he desires only the repeal of his banishment and the restoration of his lands. Throughout, he treats Richard with courtesy, although significantly he states that he will not oppose the will of heaven, whatever it might be. He later resolves to use force only if necessary: "Methinks King Richard and myself should meet/ With no less terror than the elements/ Of fire and water, when their thund'ring shock/ At meeting tears the cloudy cheeks of heaven./ Be he the fire, I'll be the yielding water" (53-57).

Here, we see Richard and Bolingbroke together for the first time since Bolingbroke's banishment in Act I, Scene 3. The positions of power in the first act have now been reversed; Bolingbroke clearly has the upper hand. Richard is again associated with the sun when Bolingbroke gazes upward and notices his appearance on the castle walls: "King Richard doth himself appear,/ As doth the blushing discontented sun/ From out the fiery portal of the East,/ When he perceives the envious clouds are bent/ To dim his glory" (61-65). As York subsequently observes, he still retains the appearance of a king, yet his glory will soon be a thing of the past.

Indeed, Richard's long speech that follows is a last moment of dignity and grandeur as sovereign. When Richard speaks, he addresses the abrasive and disrespectful Northumberland rather than Bolingbroke, who stands a distance away. He recovers his majestic tone and again asserts his authority as the "lawful king." He refers with thinly veiled sarcasm to his divine right: "If we be not [King], show us the hand of God/ That hath dismissed us from our stewardship" (76-77). His claims are reinforced by the presence of the Bishop of Carlisle. Note that here and elsewhere the clergymen have allied with Richard rather than with Bolingbroke.

Again, we are greeted by a prophecy when Richard proclaims

that civil war will ensue if Bolingbroke seizes the crown. Here, Richard casts off the self-pitying posture of the previous scene to assert his rights as hereditary king, enthroned by the grace of God. He criticizes Bolingbroke as an ungodly usurper and predicts: "But ere the crown he looks for live in peace,/ Ten thousand bloody crowns of mothers' sons/ Shall ill become the flower of England's face" (94-96). Yet Northumberland, in his reply, stresses that Bolingbroke is also a grandson of King Edward III when he refers to … "the royalties of both your bloods" (106).

The scene is noteworthy for its use of physical contrast emphasis in the positioning of Richard and his remaining allies and Bolingbroke and his army. Richard stands high—in Shakespeare's theatre he would have stood on the balcony or second level of the stage—while Bolingbroke and his men occupy the forestage below.

When Northumberland relates Bolingbroke's pledge that he desires only the repealment of his banishment and his "lineal royalties" and will then "beg/ Infranchisement immediate on his knees" and lay down his arms, swearing allegience to the crown, Richard promptly grants his request. Yet he has a perverse change of heart immediately afterward. He tells Aumerle that he has debased himself; overcome with grief, he proclaims: "O God! O God! that e'er this tongue of mine,/ That laid the sentence of dread banishment/ On yon proud man, should take it off again/ With words of sooth!" (132-135).

Inexplicably, before Northumberland can deliver Bolingbroke's response to the King's pledge (which may, in fact, be a promise of loyalty and good behavior), it is Richard who brings up the idea of deposition. Clearly, Richard sees through Bolingbroke's public pronouncements of what he claims to be seeking by his insurrection. Yet Bolingbroke's reply is never made known. Again, Richard's tone is rife with self-pity. He is more interested in contemplating his downfall than in listening to Bolingbroke's response to his pardon. He revels in perverse self-display as his thoughts turn eloquently, albeit grimly, to his expectations for the future. Here again, he is the poet-philosopher, self-consciously surveying his feelings of desolation and comparing his past to the destiny he anticipates—the renouncement of his worldly goods, an austere holy life, and ultimately, a lonely death: "I'll give my jewels for a set of beads;/ My gorgeous palace for a hermitage;/ My gay apparel for an almsman's gown;/ My figured goblets for a dish of wood,/ My sceptre for a palmer's walking staff;/ My subjects for a pair of carvèd saints;/ And my large kingdom for a little grave" (146-152).

Even so, Richard retains enough self-possession to comfort the weeping Aumerle. Although he despairs over his fate, he is boldly defiant when he submits to Northumberland's demand that he meet with Bolingbroke in "the base court." When he cries, "Down, down I come, like glist'ring Phaethon/ Wanting the manage of unruly jades," he is alluding to classical mythology and the recurring motif of the sun as a royal emblem (177-178). Phaethon, an unwise young man half-mortal and half-god, drove his father Apollo's sun chariot but was unable to command the horses that drew it and plunged wildly out of control. Zeus, seeing his erratic flight across the heavens, struck him down with a thunderbolt to save the world from destruction. Here, Richard acknowledges that his downfall resulted from a similar inability to manage his kingdom.

The descent from the ramparts that follows is rife with symbolism, for when Richard emerges on the mainstage he and Bolingbroke are on level ground. Although Bolingbroke kneels politely when the King emerges from the castle and maintains a posture of reverence toward his sovereign, Richard quickly punctures the myth of his pledge of loyalty when he remarks that Bolingbroke's ambitions are "thus high"—meaning, of course, his crown, which he indicates by a gesture. In defeat, he maintains his dignity and is gravely courteous to his adversaries, but he recognizes his own powerlessness when he tells Bolingbroke, "What you will have, I'll give, and willing too,/ For do we must what force will have us do" (204-205).

Act III, Scene 4

New Characters:

Ladies-in-Waiting: *attendants to the Queen*

Gardeners: *servants to the Duke of York*

Summary

This scene takes place in the Duke of York's garden. The Queen asks her Ladies-in-Waiting, "What sport shall we devise here in this garden,/ To drive away the heavy thought of care?" (1-2). One of the Ladies suggests lawn bowling or dancing, but the Queen is in no mood for either diversion. The Lady then suggests telling tales and volunteers to sing for the Queen. However, the Queen, feeling sorrowful, refuses her offer.

Three Gardeners enter, one the master, the other two his men. The Queen and her attendants stand aside and eavesdrop on their conversation; the Queen anticipates that they will talk about England's recent problems. The Master Gardener bids one of his men to bind up the dangling apricots "Which like unruly children make their sire/ Stoop with oppression of their prodigal weight," and bids the second man to "like an executioner/ Cut off the heads of too fast growing sprays/ That look too lofty in our common-wealth:/ All must be even in our government" (30-31; 33-36). While they are at their tasks, the Master Gardener will "root away/ The noisome weeds which without profit suck/ The soil's fertility from wholesome flowers" (37-39).

One of the men wonders why the Gardeners should "keep law and form and due proportion" when England itself "Is full of weeds, her fairest flowers choked up,/ Her fruit trees all unpruned, her hedges ruined/ …and her wholesome herbs/ Swarming with cat-erpillars?" (41; 44-47). The Master Gardener replies that the sover-eign responsible for this disorder has "now himself met with the fall of leaf," and that the "weeds which his broad spreading leaves did shelter"—the Earl of Wiltshire, Bushy, and Green—have been "plucked up root and all by Bolingbroke" (49-53). He adds that Bolingbroke has seized "the wasteful King" and remarks that it is a pity that King Richard did not treat his realm with the care the Gardeners have lavished upon their garden. The King, he com-ments, has already suffered a reversal of fortune and will doubt-less be deposed.

Hearing this news, the Queen steps forward and addresses the Master Gardener; she chastises him for saying that the King has been deposed and asks how he came by these ill tidings. The Gar-dener tells her he has taken little joy in this news, but he assures

her it is true, and indeed, has become common knowledge: King Richard has been captured by Bolingbroke, who now has the allegience of "all the English peers."

The Queen is distraught when she realizes she is the last to learn of her husband's misfortune. She orders her Ladies-in-Waiting to accompany her to London, where she will meet the King. Before she departs, she remarks, "Gard'ner, for telling me these news of woe,/ Pray God, the plants thou graft'st may never grow" (100-101). After she is gone, the Gardener resolves to plant a bank of rue—the herb of sorrow—at the spot where one of the Queen's tears fell.

Analysis

At the beginning of this scene, the Queen finds that there is no consolation for the pain she is feeling. Her comments to her Gentlewomen echo the Duchess of Gloucester's woe at the death of her husband and Bolingbroke's sorrow at his impending exile in Act I, Scene 3; the Gentlewomen are of as little comfort as Gaunt was to his sister-in-law and his son.

In the Master Gardener's instructions to his men, we again hear a series of metaphors used many times earlier in the play. In Act II, Scene 1, for example, John of Gaunt referred to England as "this blessed plot, this earth" (50) and alluded to himself as a "too-long-withered flower" (134). Here, the metaphors of soil, gardening, and harmful insects are extended and developed more fully. England, the Master Gardener argues, has "noisome weeds" and "superfluous branches" which must be rooted and lopped off if the rest of the kingdom is to prosper; we behold the disorder of the kingdom in miniature. When he refers to caterpillars—instruments of a garden's destruction—it recalls Bolingbroke's reference to Bushy and Bagot as "The caterpillars of the commonwealth,/ Which I have sworn to weed and pluck away." (II, iii, 165-166)

This extended parable gives the audience (or the reader) time to reflect before the deposition scene soon to come. The Master Gardener comments directly on Richard's policies: "O, what pity is it/ That he had not so trimmed and dressed his land/ As we this garden! ...Had he done so, himself had borne the crown,/ Which waste of idle hours hath quite thrown down" (55-57; 65-66).

Ironically, the Queen is the last to know of the King's capture and imminent deposition. Her references to the Garden of Eden recall Gaunt's similar analogy in Act II, Scene 1. Yet here, Richard has assumed a central place in a cosmic tragedy; like Adam, his transgressions have resulted in the loss of a kingdom granted by divine authority.

Study Questions

1. Which two characters does Bolingbroke order to be executed?

2. What reasons does Bolingbroke give for these executions?

3. Why does King Richard believe that Bolingbroke's rebellion will fail?

4. Where does Richard resolve to seek refuge from Bolingbroke's forces?

5. Who shares Richard's refuge?

6. What does Bolingbroke claim as his purpose in confronting the King with his army?

7. What does King Richard anticipate if he submits to Bolingbroke?

8. What is Bolingbroke's first response when the King comes down from the walls of the castle?

9. What diversions does the Queen's Lady-in-Waiting suggest to cheer her spirits?

10. What herb does the Gardener promise to plant at the spot where one of the Queen's tears fell?

Answers

1. Bolingbroke orders the executions of Bushy and Green.

2. Bolingbroke asserts that Bushy and Green have misled the King and caused a breach between the King and Queen. He also claims that they made the King misinterpret him and subsequently pillaged his estate.

3. Richard maintains that Bolingbroke's rebellion will fail because he is king by divine right. He comments that "Not all the water in the rough rude sea/ Can wash the balm off from an annointed king;/ The breath of worldly men cannot depose/ The deputy elected by the Lord."

4. King Richard decides to seek refuge from Bolingbroke's forces at Flint Castle in Wales.

5. The King is accompanied to Flint Castle by the Duke of Aumerle, the Earl of Salisbury, Sir Stephen Scroop, and the Bishop of Carlisle.

6. Bolingbroke claims that he will swear "allegiance and true faith of heart" to the King and lay at his feet his "arms and power" if the King will repeal his banishment and restore his lands.

7. King Richard anticipates that if he submits to Bolingbroke he will be deposed and reduced to the status of a commoner. He also anticipates his own death and burial in "an obscure grave."

8. When King Richard comes down from the walls of Flint Castle, Bolingbroke commands his nobles and soldiers to "show fair duty to his Majesty." He kneels before Richard and addresses him as "My gracious Lord."

9. The Queen's Lady-in-Waiting suggests lawn bowling, dancing, and storytelling; she also volunteers to sing.

10. The Gardener promises to plant a bed of rue, the herb of sorrow, at the spot where one of the Queen's tears fell.

Suggested Essay Topics

1. Compare and contrast King Richard's poetic eloquence when faced with defeat with his language and behavior in earlier scenes.

2. Discuss the possible reasons for the Duke of York's defection to Bolingbroke's cause.

3. Examine the validity of Bolingbroke's claim that he is seeking only the restoration of his title and lands.

4. Explore the ways in which the nature analogies made by the Gardeners reflect conditions in England in the recent past.

Act IV

Act IV, Scene 1

New Characters:

Lord Fitzwater: *a nobleman who accuses the Duke of Aumerle of treason*

Duke of Surrey: *a nobleman who defends the Duke of Aumerle*

Abbot of Westminster: *a clergyman who plots against Henry Bolingbroke*

Summary

At Westminster Hall in London, Bolingbroke and the nobles of the realm gather in Parliament. Among those in attendance are the Duke of Aumerle, the Earl of Northumberland, Harry Percy, Lord Fitzwater, and the Duke of Surrey. Also present are two clergymen: the Bishop of Carlisle and the Abbot of Westminster. The issue of the crown is now to be decided, but Bolingbroke has first scheduled an inquest into the Duke of Gloucester's murder. Bolingbroke commands that Sir William Bagot be brought forth. When Bagot enters Bolingbroke asks him to confess what he knows about Gloucester's death—specifically who persuaded the King to order his assassination, and who actually killed him. "Then set before my face the Lord Aumerle," Bagot replies (6). Aumerle steps forward and Bagot accuses him of boasting that he could assassinate Gloucester at the time the murder was being planned. Bagot also states that Aumerle declared he would refuse the offer of a

hundred thousand crowns rather than see Bolingbroke return to England; furthermore, Aumerle had remarked that England would be blessed if Bolingbroke died in exile.

Aumerle vehemently denies the charges; he hurls down his gage and calls Bagot a liar. Bolingbroke commands that Bagot not pick up the gage to accept Aumerle's challenge. However, Lord Fitzwater hurls down his own gage to challenge Aumerle; he claims that he, too, heard Aumerle confess he was responsible for Gloucester's murder. Aumerle calls Fitzwater a coward, and Harry Percy protests that Aumerle is a liar; he throws down his gage to challenge Aumerle and is seconded by one of Bolingbroke's Lords. Aumerle replies boldly that he is ready to accept twenty thousand challenges.

The Duke of Surrey remarks that he was present when Fitzwater and Aumerle spoke. Fitzwater admits that Surrey's statement is true, and that Surrey can confirm his accusation. But Surrey calls Fitzwater's charge a falsehood. Fitzwater, in turn, calls Surrey a liar. Surrey hurls down his gage as a challenge and Fitzwater accepts. He protests that Aumerle is indeed responsible for Gloucester's murder. He adds that he heard the banished Thomas Mowbray confess that Aumerle sent two of his men to accomplish the killing. Aumerle protests that Mowbray is a liar and challenges the banished Mowbray in absentia.

Bolingbroke proclaims that the various challenges will "rest under gage" until Mowbray returns from exile. He pledges that in time Mowbray's banishment will end and remarks that although Mowbray is his enemy, he will be "restored again/ To all his lands" (88-89). But the Bishop of Carlisle announces that Mowbray, who after his banishment fought valiantly in the Crusades, had since retired to Italy where he died peacefully. Bolingbroke speaks with kindness of his former adversary and commands that the differences between Aumerle and his challengers will be set aside until he can assign the contentious nobles a day of trial by combat.

The Duke of York enters and announces that King Richard, "with willing soul," has agreed to yield up his "high sceptre" to Bolingbroke. York tells Bolingbroke to ascend the throne and proclaims, "Long live Henry, fourth of that name!" Bolingbroke replies, "In God's name, I'll ascend the regal throne" (112-113). But the

Bishop of Carlisle immediately objects: "Marry, God forbid!" He proceeds to explain his reasoning. "What subject," he asks, "can give sentence on his king?/ And who sits here that is not Richard's subject?" (121-122). He also states that it is a "black, obscene" deed for a King who has ruled by divine right to be judged by those of "inferior breath," particularly when he is not present. He announces to the Parliament that "My Lord of Hereford here, whom you call king,/ Is a foul traitor.../ And if you crown him, let me prophesy/ The blood of English shall manure the ground,/ And future ages groan for this foul act" (134-138). He predicts that civil war and "disorder, horror, fear, and mutiny" will follow for years to come if Bolingbroke usurps the throne.

Northumberland promptly orders the Bishop arrested for capital treason and commands that the Abbot of Westminster hold him as prisoner until he can be tried. Bolingbroke then issues the command for King Richard to be brought to Parliament so that he might formally surrender the crown "in common view." The Duke of York exits to bring Richard before the assembly.

A moment later, York returns with Richard, who laments that he has been called before his successor "Before I have shook off the regal thoughts/ Wherewith I reigned" (163-164). He remarks that those assembled had once cried "all hail" to him, but now they have betrayed him as Judas betrayed Christ. He asks York why he has been summoned; York replies that he must now "do that office of thine own good will,/ Which tired majesty did make thee offer:/ the resignation of thy state and crown/ To Henry Bolingbroke" (177-180).

"Give me the crown," Richard commands. He holds it out to Bolingbroke and remarks scornfully: "Here, cousin, seize the crown." They hold it together a moment, and then Richard reluctantly abdicates the throne with an elaborate public display of regal grief. He concludes with a flourish: "God save King Henry, unkinged Richard says,/ And send him many years of sunshine days" (219-220). He then asks, "What more remains?" Northumberland tells Richard he must read the accusations against him and confess to his crimes and those of his courtiers so that "the souls of men/ Might deem that you are worthily deposed" (225-226).

However, Richard protests that his eyes are too full of tears to read, although he can clearly see "traitors here." He asks Bolingbroke to order a mirror brought to the Parliament chamber. Northumberland again asks Richard to read the list of charges against him while awaiting the mirror, but Bolingbroke mercifully tells Northumberland to "urge it no more."

An attendant enters with the mirror soon afterward, and Richard gazes sorrowfully upon his own features: "Was this the face/ That, like the sun, did make the beholders wink?" (282-283). Realizing that his features are no longer those of a king, and profoundly saddened by what he sees, he hurls the mirror down, breaking it. He then asks Bolingbroke's permission to leave the Parliament chamber. Bolingbroke orders his Lords to escort Richard to the Tower of London, and Richard exits. Bolingbroke decrees that his own coronation will take place the following Wednesday and exits with his court. The Abbot of Westminster, the Bishop of Carlisle, and the Duke of Aumerle remain.

"A woeful pageant have we here beheld," remarks the Abbot of Westminster (320). The Bishop of Carlisle reiterates that "The woe's to come," and that future generations will suffer as a result of the events that transpired that day. Aumerle asks the clergymen, "Is there no plot/ To rid the realm of this pernicious blot?" (323-324). The Abbot of Westminster replies that he does indeed have a scheme in mind, and he invites Aumerle to supper to discuss his plan.

Analysis

The beginning of this act, which contains only a single scene, parallels in many ways the conflicts and challenges of Act I, Scene 1. This time, however, it is Bolingbroke who sits in judgement. Although Bolingbroke has not been crowned, he is clearly acting as king. Again, we are greeted by accusations, counter accusations, and gages hurled down in anger; again, the principal issue is the Duke of Gloucester's murder.

It is, of course, politically expedient for Bolingbroke to confirm that his original accusations against Mowbray—and by extension, the King himself—were truthful. By establishing that Richard did, in fact, have a hand in Gloucester's death, and that his subsequent banishment of Bolingbroke and the seizure of Gaunt's lands were unjust, Bolingbroke will be solidifying his claim to the throne. Yet Bolingbroke succeeds in arbitrating the conflicts among his Lords no better than Richard did in the first act, and the truth of the various accusations is never revealed. Like his predecessor, Bolingbroke can only decree that the issues raised by the contending noblemen will be put off "Till we assign you to your days of trial" (106).

Nevertheless, Bolingbroke is again revealed as a crafty politician—note that he originally planned to defer judgement until Mowbray's return from exile, which could occur only by his royal decree. His mood throughout this scene is one of repressed, kingly dignity; he also curries favor with the nobles by his merciful promise to pardon a former enemy, even before he learns that Mowbray has died in Italy.

As audiences in Shakespeare's time knew, the Bishop of Carlisle's prediction that if Bolingbroke is crowned the result will be civil war and bloodshed was accurate; civil war would ensue early in the new king's reign, and Bolingbroke's grandson, King Henry VI, would later be deposed in the War of the Roses, a conflict between the noble English houses of Lancaster and York. Not until 1485, when King Henry VII ascended the throne, would the conflict ultimately be resolved.

Note that Northumberland does much of the dirty work for his future sovereign. For example, it is Northumberland, rather than the new king, who orders Carlisle's arrest for treason. Bolingbroke gives no direct indication that he has been affected by Carlisle's prophecy, yet his next words are significant: he orders Richard to be brought to the Parliament chamber to surrender the crown "in common view" so that he might then "proceed without suspicion." Indeed, the entire proceeding is a public spectacle arranged by Bolingbroke to legitimize his claim to the throne.

When Richard arrives to formally renounce his "state and crown" he again compares himself to Christ betrayed by Judas in an effort to castigate his foes; later, he compares himself to Christ at his trial before Pilate. Here again, he is referring to his divine right and anticipating his own martyrdom; he asserts that the rejection of God's annointed is being enacted once again. He is profoundly saddened by the necessity of surrendering his crown, but he realizes that it is the only course available to him. Yet he abdicates with reluctance; he stresses at every opportunity the fact that he is being forcefully and unlawfully deposed. He seizes the moment to dramatize his abdication before a Parliament that had until recently obeyed his commands: "Now, mark me how I will undo myself" (202). When Northumberland asks Richard to read the charges against him, he makes an elaborate show of defiant refusal; in doing so, he makes it clear that he considers Bolingbroke a traitorous usurper.

Soon afterward, we are greeted by yet another reference to the sun, but this time it is a reversal of earlier imagery: Richard proclaims, "O, that I were a mockery king of snow,/ Standing before the sun of Bolingbroke/ To melt myself away in water drops" (259-261). His tone has shifted from defiance to one of indulgent self-pity, but he is eloquent in expressing his feelings. Yet here, as elsewhere, he is conscious not only of his own emotions, but also that he is performing for the assembled nobles.

This scene contains two striking moments of visual drama. The first occurs when Richard asks for the crown, then holds it forth to Bolingbroke; both men grasp it for a moment as Richard stage manages the symbolic transfer of power. Later, when Richard, after gazing sadly at his reflection, smashes the mirror brought at his request, it creates an equally striking stage picture. This is, of course, a grand gesture on the part of the former king; he is genuinely saddened, yet he also realizes that his action is ripe with symbolism. Bolingbroke, too, recognizes the dual nature of Richard's gesture. As he comments: "The shadow of your sorrow hath destroyed/ The shadow of your face" (291-292). Here, he accuses Richard of merely putting on an outward show of grief. Richard is momentarily taken aback by his remark, yet he quickly acknowledges that his "grief lies all within,/ And these external manners of laments/ Are merely shadows to the unseen grief/ That swells with silence in the tortured soul" (294-297).

As this scene nears its end, the transfer of power is complete; Bolingbroke looks forward to his coronation, and Richard is led away to prison. But as we learn just before the conclusion, a threat has arisen to the new king in the form of the conspiracy hatched by the Abbot of Westminster—a plot to which the Duke of Aumerle will soon become an accomplice. Thus, Shakespeare introduces further dramatic complications as the fourth act draws to a close.

Study Questions

1. What charges does Sir William Bagot bring against the Duke of Aumerle?

2. Which noblemen support Bagot's charges?

3. Who defends Aumerle against the accusations that are made?

4. What does the Bishop of Carlisle predict if Bolingbroke is crowned as King Henry IV?

5. What is the Earl of Northumberland's response to the Bishop of Carlisle's prophecy?

6. What does the Duke of York tell Richard when he asks why Bolingbroke has sent for him?

7. What object does King Richard request after his abdication and what does he do with this object?

8. Where does Bolingbroke order that Richard is to be held as prisoner?

9. When does Bolingbroke announce that his coronation will take place?

10. Who instigates a plot against the new king?

Answers

1. Bagot accuses the Duke of Aumerle of plotting the Duke of Gloucester's murder. He also accuses Aumerle of swearing he would refuse the offer of a hundred thousand crowns rather than see Bolingbroke's return to England, and he claims Aumerle had declared that England would be "blest" if Bolingbroke died in exile.

2. Lord Fitzwater, Harry Percy, and an unnamed Lord support Bagot's accusations.

3. The Duke of Surrey defends Aumerle.

4. The Bishop of Carlisle prophesies civil war and bloodshed for generations to come if Bolingbroke is crowned.

5. The Earl of Northumberland orders the Bishop of Carlisle's arrest for high treason.

6. York tells King Richard that he has been summoned before Bolingbroke and the Parliament "To do that office of thine own good will,/ Which tired majesty did make thee offer:/ The resignation of thy state and crown/ To Henry Bolingbroke."

7. King Richard requests a mirror after his abdication. After gazing at his reflection, he hurls the mirror to the ground, shattering it into "a hundred shivers."

8. Bolingbroke commands that Richard is to be held prisoner in the Tower of London.

9. Bolingbroke decrees that his coronation as King Henry IV will take place the next Wednesday.

10. The Abbot of Westminster instigates a plot against King Henry IV.

Suggested Essay Topics

1. Compare the accusations and challenges early in the fourth act and Bolingbroke's management of his contentious nobles to the similar accusations and challenges in Act I, Scene 1 and King Richard's handling of the situation.

2. Discuss and analyze King Richard's behavior in the fourth act—to what extent are his emotions genuine and to what extent is he play-acting for the benefit of those assembled in Parliament?

3. You are a newspaper reporter assigned to cover the momentous events in Parliament on the day King Richard's deposition takes place. Write a news story about these events; try to be as fair as possible. Your story should also include commentary and analysis. What do these extraordinary events mean for England's future?

4. Compare and contrast Shakespeare's account of the events
   in Act IV with the account of these incidents in Holinshed's
   Chronicles, Shakespeare's principal source for *Richard II*. (An
   abridged version is available in many paperback editions of
   the play.) How and why did Shakespeare depart from his
   source material?

Act V

Act V, Scene 1

Summary

Scene 1 takes place on a street in London. We encounter the Queen and her attendants; the Queen comments that King Richard will pass that way as he is led to the Tower of London, where he has been sent as a prisoner by "proud Bolingbroke." Richard enters, accompanied by a Guard, and the Queen laments the circumstances to which he has been reduced. When Richard sees his Queen he counsels her to "Join not with grief, fair woman," but rather to "think our former state a happy dream,/ From which awaked, the truth of what we are/ Shows us but this" (16; 18-20). He tells the Queen he is "sworn brother" to "grim necessity" and urges her to seek refuge in a convent in France. Only through leading a holy life, he remarks, will they be able to redeem themselves.

The Queen is startled to find her husband "transformed and weakened." She entreats him not to take "correction mildly," but rather to react with the anger of one who has been a powerful king. Richard again bids her to journey to France. "Think I am dead," he comments. He tells her to consider their meeting a final parting and asks her to tell the woeful tale of his deposition to those she will encounter in years to come.

Northumberland enters and delivers the news that Bolingbroke has changed his mind about where Richard will be imprisoned; he must now proceed to Pomfret Castle, and the Queen will immediately be banished to her native France. Richard chastises

Northumberland as the "ladder wherewithal/ The mounting Bolingbroke ascends my throne" (55-56). He predicts that in the future King Henry's reign will be plagued by corruption, and that a rift will develop between Northumberland and his sovereign. But Northumberland brusquely tells the King that the hour has arrived when he must part with his Queen. Upset by this news, the Queen asks Northumberland if Richard can share her banishment, or she his imprisonment. But Richard realizes, sadly yet pragmatically, that they now must go their separate ways. They exchange a tender parting kiss and exit, Richard to prison, and his Queen to exile in France.

Analysis

Although the Queen has appeared in three earlier scenes and we have learned of her devotion to Richard, this is the first time we have seen her in intimate conversation with her husband. This poignant scene illustrates the depth of their affection and their reduced status in the commonwealth; they are no longer king and queen, but rather two private citizens bidding a sad farewell.

Richard, as he is being led to prison, accepts his fate with dignified resignation. The Queen, on the other hand, is irate at his passivity, commenting: "The lion dying thrusteth forth his paw/ And wounds the earth, if nothing else, with rage/ To be o'erpow'red" (29-31). The comparison of Richard to a lion is one we have heard earlier; in Act I, Scene 1, Richard commented, referring to himself: "Lions make leopards tame." Similarly, the Queen's reference to seeing "My fair rose wither" (8) recalls the Gardeners' scene and the many images of flowers and gardens throughout the play. It is ironic, however, when the Queen compares Richard to a "most beauteous inn" and Bolingbroke to an ordinary "alehouse guest," for Bolingbroke's popularity with the common people assisted his rise to the throne.

It is also ironic when Richard tells Northumberland that he will soon rebel against King Henry; as Shakespeare's audience knew, Northumberland would in fact lead an uprising against his sovereign. Shakespeare later dramatized this rebellion in *Henry IV, Part I*. Although the Queen pleads for Richard to accompany her into exile, Richard is aware that Bolingbroke, a pragmatic politician, won't allow this to occur. As he comments, it would be of "some love, but little policy" (84). Bolingbroke, of course, had been exiled and later returned to seize the crown. Thus, Richard and his Queen are forced to part tenderly before the former king is led off to prison.

Act V, Scene 2

New Character:

Duchess of York: *wife to Edmund, Duke of York; mother of the Duke of Aumerle*

Summary

At the Duke of York's palace, the Duke has been recounting the story of Bolingbroke's triumphant entry into London when he has been forced to break off his tale by his own tears. The common people, he told his wife, had thrown "dust and rubbish" at King Richard's head as he was led captive through the streets. Bolingbroke had been cheered by the crowd yet "no joyful tongue" welcomed Richard home. Nevertheless, Richard had endured his demeaning journey with dignity. York assures his wife that "heaven hath a hand in these events," and he reminds her that as loyal subjects of the crown their allegiance is now to Bolingbroke (37).

The Duke of Aumerle enters; he is in a despairing mood over the fate of King Richard. The Duchess inquires who the new favorites are at court, but Aumerle tells his mother that he doesn't know and doesn't care. When York asks his son whether tournaments at Oxford to celebrate King Henry's accession will be held, Aumerle replies cryptically that they will and that he will be there "if God prevent me not."

Suddenly York notices a letter tucked into Aumerle's gown and asks to see it. Aumerle refuses, telling his father it is "a matter of small consequence." But York is suspicious; he grabs the letter away from his son and glances at it. He is livid at the contents. "Treason, foul treason, villain, traitor, slave!" he exclaims, now knowing that his son is among those who plan to assassinate King Henry (72). He shouts for a servant to saddle his horse so that he might journey immediately to the King.

The Duchess is mystified by her husband's reaction and urges Aumerle to strike his father. She realizes that Aumerle is involved in a treacherous plot; however, she is determined to protect her only son, even if it means a breach with her husband. But the Duke, furious, tells her that Aumerle is among a dozen conspirators who have pledged to kill King Henry at Oxford. The Duchess protests that they can keep Aumerle at home so he will not have an opportunity to participate in the scheme. But York, determined to reveal his son's part in the conspiracy, storms out over the Duchess's protests. The Duchess urges Aumerle to ride swiftly to the King and to plead for his mercy before York can accuse his son of treason. She pledges to follow him and tells him, "Never will I rise up from the ground/ Till Bolingbroke have pardoned thee" (116-117).

Analysis

At the beginning of this scene we are again reminded of Richard's humiliating reversal of fortune. York's vivid account of the new king being acclaimed by the crowd, and of the people of London heaping dust and rubbish on Richard's head as he was led through the streets, is genuinely poignant; Richard, formerly a capricious and shallow monarch, is again cast in a sympathetic light. Again, we are greeted by a theatrical analogy when York tells his wife that after Bolingbroke's triumphant entrance, Richard was treated rudely by the assembled crowd: "As in a theatre the eyes of men,/ After a well-graced actor leaves the stage,/ Are idly bent on him that enters next,/ Thinking his prattle to be tedious;/ Even so, or with much more contempt, men's eyes/ Did scowl on gentle Richard" (23-28).

When York discovers the letter his son has concealed, we learn that the murderous plot devised at the end of Act IV has now been implemented. York, loyal to the crown, has sworn his allegiance to the new monarch, despite his sympathy for Richard. He is furious to learn that his son is implicated in the conspiracy. In Act II, Scene 1 (171-183), York chastised Richard for lacking the virtues of his noble father; here, he finds much the same failing in his own son. Aumerle, on the other hand, has maintained the personal loyalty to Richard he has demonstrated throughout the play. In Act III, Scene 3, for example, he revealed his devotion to Richard by his tears when he learned that the King's downfall was imminent. York's exit to bring news of the plot to King Henry, Aumerle's hasty attempt to get to the King first, and the Duchess's promise to follow prepare the way for the presence of all three characters in the ensuing scene.

Act V, Scene 3

Summary

At Windsor Castle, we encounter Bolingbroke, now King Henry IV, along with Harry Percy and other noblemen. Bolingbroke asks if any of his courtiers have heard news of his son, Prince Hal. He has not seen his son in three months; usually, he remarks, Hal is to be found in taverns consorting with "loose companions" and thieves. Percy replies that he had seen the Prince two days earlier and had told him of the forthcoming jousts at Oxford. Hal retorted that he would go to a brothel to obtain a prostitute's glove as a good luck token, and with that he would "unhorse the lustiest challenger." Bolingbroke is unsurprised by Hal's response, yet he is confident that his dissolute heir will change for the better as he grows older.

Suddenly, Aumerle bursts into the royal chamber and pleads for a word alone with the King. Percy and the other Lords depart; after they exit, Aumerle falls to his knees and begs for mercy, without explaining his offense. The King pledges that if his sin is "intended" rather than committed—however heinous it might be—he will issue a pardon. Aumerle asks permission to lock the door and Henry grants it. But as soon as Aumerle turns the key the Duke of York is heard banging on the door with a dire warning: "My liege, beware …/ Thou hast a traitor in thy presence there" (38-39).

Bolingbroke promptly draws his sword and threatens to kill Aumerle, but Aumerle assures him he has nothing to fear. York, in the meantime, has continued to shout that a traitor is within. Bolingbroke opens the door. York enters, and Bolingbroke asks him the cause of his excitement. York hands the King the letter he seized from his son and asks him to read it. Aumerle implores the King to remember his promise of a pardon and tells him he has repented: "Read not my name there;/ My heart is not confederate with my hand" (51-52). York tells the King that his son is motivated by fear and not by loyalty; he urges the King to forego his royal mercy.

Bolingbroke is startled to learn of the conspiracy against his life; he is dismayed that the son of the loyal Duke of York is involved. York tells the King he is ashamed of his son, but his speech is interrupted when the Duchess shouts at the door, begging to be admitted to the royal chamber. Bolingbroke tells his "dangerous cousin" to let her in. Aumerle unlocks the door. The Duchess enters, falls to her knees, and begs for her son's life. Aumerle, too, falls to his knees, echoing his mother's plea. The Duke of York kneels as well, but he urges the King to deal harshly with his son.

Bolingbroke, after listening to the Duchess's entreaties, proclaims that he will pardon Aumerle "as God pardons me." The Duchess is overjoyed at his magnanimity, but the King promises that the other conspirators will be captured and executed. He orders the Duke of York to lead soldiers to Oxford, or wherever the conspirators have assembled, to suppress the plot. He also expresses the hope that the Duke of Aumerle has truly reformed. The Duchess tells her son, "I pray God make thee new," and she leads Aumerle away.

Analysis

Bolingbroke's reference to his wastrel son at the beginning of this scene would have provoked immediate signs of recognition in Shakespeare's audience. Prince Hal was a legendary figure in Elizabethan England; although by tradition he spent much of his youth in the company of "loose companions," he later became King Henry V, one of England's most honored warrior-kings. Shakespeare would later tell his story in *Henry IV, Parts I and II* and *Henry V.*

The arrival of Aumerle, followed by his father and then his mother, is a logical continuation of the previous scene. The confusion of their conflicting stories is almost comic; even Bolingbroke proclaims after the Duchess's arrival: "Our scene is alt'red from a serious thing,/ And now changed to 'The Beggar and the King'" (78-79). Bolingbroke, although shaken by news of the conspiracy, is merciful to the son of an ally whose neutrality and ultimate support meant a good deal to his cause. The Duchess's praise of the new king after he pardons her son—"A God on earth thou art"—

reveals that Richard's role as "God's annointed" has now been effectively transferred (135).

Earlier, of course, Bolingbroke had been similarly magnanimous to Mowbray, his former enemy, before learning that Mowbray had died in Italy. He doubtless realized that Aumerle, isolated from his co-conspirators, presented little threat, and that his own tenuous claim to the throne might be solidified by an act of generosity toward his cousin, whose loyal father was the last surviving son of King Edward III. His generosity is by no means universal, however, as we will see in scenes to come.

Act V, Scenes 4 and 5

New Characters:

Sir Pierce of Exton: *a knight loyal to King Henry IV*

Groom: *a stable hand who formerly tended King Richard's horses*

Keeper: *a jailer at Pomfret Castle*

Summary

In another part of Windsor Castle, Sir Pierce of Exton remarks to a Servant that twice he had heard the King say, "Have I no friend will rid me of this living fear?" (2). He was referring, of course, to Richard, and to the possibility that he might somehow regain his crown. The Servant confirms that Exton had heard the King correctly. Bolingbroke, Exton comments, had "wishtly looked on me" when he spoke those words, as if to imply that Exton had been selected to kill Richard. "I am the King's friend," Exton resolves, "and will rid his foe" (11).

In Scene 5, which takes place in Richard's prison cell at Pomfret Castle, the former king, in a philosophical mood, reflects upon his present situation. He muses on his imprisonment, with all the contradictory thoughts it has evoked. He would like to tear his way out of his cell but realizes he cannot; he then comforts himself with the thought that he is not the first to suffer misfortune. He thinks back to the days when he was King, yet he cannot forget the more recent circumstances of his deposition and is saddened by his memories.

Music is heard, and Richard remarks, "How sour sweet music is/ When time is broke, and no proportion kept;/ So is it in the music of men's lives" (42-44). The music's rhythm leads him to reflect that "I wasted time, and now doth Time waste me" (49). Finally he cries out, "This music mads me: let it sound no more" (61). Yet he realizes that the music was probably meant for his pleasure, and pronounces "blessing on his heart that gives it me," for he has seen few signs of thoughtfulness recently (64).

A groom of the stable enters and Richard hails him with kindness; he is glad to have company since the only other visitor he has had is the Keeper who brings him food. The Groom tells Richard that he has asked for special permission "To look upon my sometimes royal master's face." (75) He adds that he was heartbroken to see Bolingbroke, on coronation day, riding roan Barbary, the horse Richard rode often in the past, and a horse the groom had dressed when Richard was King. "Rode he on Barbary?" asks Richard. "Tell me, gentle friend,/ How went he under him?" The Groom replies that the horse responded to Bolingbroke "So proudly as if he disdained the ground." (81-83) Richard, heartbroken at this news, curses the horse, but forgives it when he realizes it knew no better.

A keeper enters with a meal for Richard; he orders the Groom to leave. Richard, too, reluctantly commands the Groom to go, and the Groom exits. The keeper asks Richard to begin his meal, but Richard asks him to taste it first to assure that no poison is present, as he has customarily done in the past. The keeper replies that he has been ordered not to taste the meal by Sir Pierce of Exton, who "lately came from the King." Richard, enraged when he realizes the meal may be poisoned, proclaims, "The devil take Henry of Lancaster, and thee!/ Patience is stale, and I am weary of it" (102-103). He attacks the keeper, who shouts for help.

Sir Pierce of Exton and his armed accomplices rush into the chamber, but Richard, in a fury, grabs one of their weapons and kills one, then another of Exton's men. But he is outnumbered, and Exton strikes him down. Richard, mortally wounded, pronounces a curse on his murderer: "That hand shall burn in never-quenching fire/ That staggers thus my person." After telling Exton that he has "with the King's blood stained the King's own land" (108-110)

he falls to the ground and dies. Exton, looking down at the lifeless form of the former king, praises Richard for his valor and prepares to bear his body to King Henry.

Analysis

Bolingbroke's comments that he would like to be rid of Richard are in sharp contrast to the mercy he has shown to Aumerle in the previous scene. Note that his wish to see Richard dead is reported by Exton rather than being spoken by Bolingbroke himself; moreover, it is expressed as a hope rather than a command. This lessens the inevitable negative impact of Richard's subsequent murder on Bolingbroke's character. Note, also, that Bolingbroke has thought of being rid of Richard only after learning of the conspiracy against his life.

Richard's soliloquy at the beginning of Scene 5 is the only moment in the play when we see him alone; his speech contains some of Shakespeare's greatest poetry. The transformation of Richard from callous sovereign to thoughtful philosopher is now complete; Shakespeare eloquently captures the soul of the deposed monarch. At first, Richard dwells upon the idea of birth and regeneration: "My brain I'll prove the female to my soul; My soul the father, and these two beget/ A generation of still-breeding thoughts/ And these same thoughts people this little world" (6-9). Significantly, he does not compare his life in prison to his former trappings of royalty, but rather to the world at large.

Richard understands that there is no escape from his confinement, and he becomes reflective as he realizes that others have suffered personal misfortune; he finds "a kind of ease" in thoughts of "such as have before endured the like" (30). In Act III, Scene 2, he had revelled in placing himself among the ranks of deposed and murdered kings; here, he identifies with the common people, specifically beggars in the stocks, thus recalling Bolingbroke's reference to "The Beggar and the King" in the previous scene, but in a more serious context.

We are again greeted by a theatrical analogy when Richard comments, "Thus play I in one person many people,/ And none contented" (31-32). At times, his thoughts have drifted to his years on the throne, and to his deposition. However, he adds that "whate'er I be/ Nor I, nor any man that but man is,/ With nothing shall he be pleased, till he be eased/ With being nothing" (38-41). Only death, he laments, will bring an end to his pain. Ironically, his own death is soon to come.

The music, perhaps intended specifically for the former King's pleasure, instead reminds him of "How sour sweet music is/ When time is broke, and no proportion kept" (42-43). When Richard comments, "I wasted time, and now doth Time waste me" (49) it recalls the Gardener's earlier reference to a king whom "waste of idle hours hath quite thrown down" (III, iv, 66). He is now aware that his situation is a direct consequence of his earlier actions. His mention of "sighs, and tears, and groans" evokes his similar references in his parting with the Queen (V, i, 89). He has gained self-knowledge through experience, yet inner peace has still eluded him.

The concern of the groom for his former sovereign is a poignant reminder that Bolingbroke, though popular with the common people, has not captured every heart. Richard's wry humor in hailing the groom as a "gentle peer" and his subsequent exchange with the servant who in better times dressed his horses are further reminders of his sadly reduced situation. Both Richard and the groom seem aware that the meal the keeper bears may be Richard's last—an ominous foreshadowing of subsequent events.

When Richard, furious at his keeper's deadly mission, attacks him violently, he finally behaves as his wife had urged him to do in Act V, Scene 1: "The lion dying thrusteth forth his paw/ And wounds the earth, if nothing else, with rage/ To be o'erpow'red." (29-31) He continues in this vein after the entry of Exton and his assassins, fighting furiously with those who have come to end his life. His valiant struggles at the end prompt the admiration even of his murderer, who expresses sincere remorse: "O, would the deed were good!" (114).

Act V, Scene 6

Summary

At Windsor Castle, Bolingbroke and the Duke of York, along with noblemen and attendants, enter to a flourish of trumpets. Bolingbroke tells York that "the rebels have consumed with fire" a

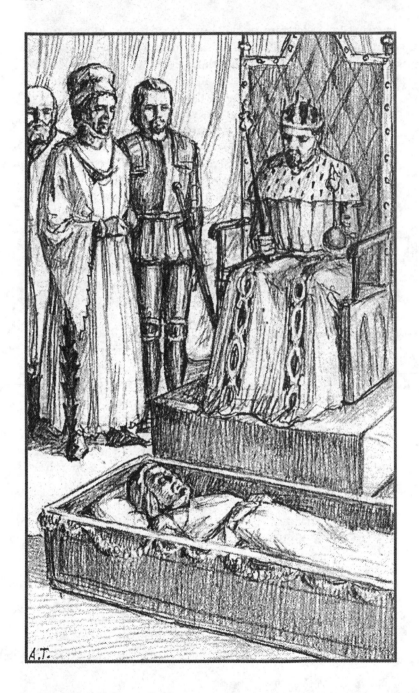

town in Gloucestershire, though he is unaware of whether the conspirators who plotted against his life have been captured or executed. The Earl of Northumberland enters and announces that
four of the conspirators have been beheaded. Lord Fitzwater arrives soon afterward with the news that two more conspirators have
been slain, then Harry Percy enters with the Bishop of Carlisle and
announces that the "grand conspirator," the Abbot of Westminster,
"With clog of conscience and sour melancholy,/ Hath yielded up
his body to the grave" (20-21). Percy urges the King to pronounce
a harsh sentence on the Bishop of Carlisle. Yet Bolingbroke mercifully sentences the Bishop to exile in a remote religious retreat
where he might live out his days in peace. He comments: "For
though mine enemy thou hast ever been,/ High sparks of honor in
thee have I seen" (28-29).

Sir Pierce of Exton enters with attendants bearing the coffin of
King Richard: "Great King, within this coffin I present/ Thy buried
fear" (30-31). Bolingbroke tells him, "Exton, I thank thee not," for
Exton has "wrought/ A deed of slander .../ Upon my head and all
this famous land" (34-36). Exton protests that he killed Richard because the King wanted him dead. But Bolingbroke replies, "though
I did wish him dead,/ I hate the murderer, love the murderèd./ The
guilt of conscience take thee for thy labor./ ...With Cain go wan-
der through shades of night,/ And never show thy head by day nor
light" (39-44). Exton exits, and Bolingbroke confesses, "Lords, I pro-
test, my soul is full of woe,/ That blood should sprinkle me to make
me grow" (45-46). He decrees that his courtiers are to dress in
mourning for King Richard, and he resolves to make a pilgrimage
to the Holy Land to atone for Richard's death.

Analysis

At the beginning of this scene we learn that the conspiracy
against the King's life in which Aumerle had initially taken part has
been suppressed. Bolingbroke's sentencing of the Bishop of
Carlisle, one of the principal conspirators, to a life of banishment
at a religious retreat is surprising, yet it has been foreshadowed by
the earlier pardon of Aumerle. His mercy toward Carlisle, like his
similar actions toward Aumerle and Mowbray, elevate his character. These acts of magnanimity, which frame the murder of King

Richard, seem illogical, yet Bolingbroke, a canny politician, doubt-less realized that he could grant amnesty to the former conspira-tors without endangering his life or his claim to the throne. Richard's death, on the other hand, was politically expedient. A liv-ing deposed king would have been a threat to the new king's secu-rity; once dead, Richard could never be the rallying point for a rebellion against the crown.

Bolingbroke's repudiation of Sir Pierce of Exton seems hypo-critical, for he had indeed expressed the wish that Richard should be killed. But he doubtless realized that distancing himself from the former king's murderer was a matter of necessity. His actions thus echo King Richard's similar renunciation of Mowbray in Act I, Scene 3. Significantly, Bolingbroke condemns Exton to endless wandering like the Biblical Cain. In Act I, Scene 1, he had accused Richard indirectly of shedding the blood of a kinsman as Cain slew Abel; as Bolingbroke realizes, he is now guilty of a similar crime.

Unlike his predecessor, however, Bolingbroke feels a genuine sense of remorse at a kinsman's murder, and he is sincere in his hope that a religious pilgrimage will in part atone for his deed. Ap-propriately, the play concludes with images of blood and tears as the new king proclaims: "I'll make a voyage to the Holy Land/ To wash this blood off from my guilty hand./ March sadly after; grace my mournings here,/ In weeping after this untimely bier" (49-52).

At the end of the play, King Henry IV is seated firmly upon the throne; Richard is dead and without heirs, and the recent conspira-cies against the life of the new monarch have been thwarted. Yet all is not well in England: King Henry has solidified his claim to the crown yet he bears the burden of an uneasy conscience. And as we know from the play's many prophecies, civil war and bloodshed will continue for years to come.

Study Questions

1. Where does King Richard urge his Queen to make her future home?

2. Where does King Henry IV send Richard to be imprisoned after changing his mind about sending him to the Tower of London?

3. What humiliations does the Duke of York tell his wife that King Richard suffered as he was led into London?

4. What information is contained in the letter the Duke of York seizes from his son?

5. What do the Duke and Duchess of York urge King Henry to do with their son, the Duke of Aumerle?

6. What duties did the Groom perform at one time for King Richard?

7. Why does the Keeper refuse to taste King Richard's food?

8. Who murders King Richard?

9. What sentence does King Henry pronounce upon the Bishop of Carlisle?

10. What does King Henry plan to do to absolve his guilt about the murder of Richard II?

Answers

1. King Richard tells the Queen to seek refuge in a convent in France.

2. King Henry revokes his order sending Richard to the Tower of London and decides to send him instead to imprisonment at Pomfret Castle.

3. The Duke of York tells his wife that King Richard, as he was being led through the streets of London, had dust and rubbish thrown on his head. York also tells his wife that Bolingbroke was cheered by the crowd, while "no joyful tongue" gave Richard "his welcome home."

4. The letter that the Duke of York seizes from his son contains information about a plot against King Henry's life and the names of the conspirators.

5. The Duke of York urges King Henry to forget his promise of a pardon and to deal harshly with his son. The Duchess begs the King to be merciful.

6. The Groom tended and dressed the King's horses.

7. The Keeper refuses to taste King Richard's food as he had in the past because he has been told not to do so by Sir Pierce of Exton.

8. Sir Pierce of Exton murders King Richard.

9. King Henry commands that the Bishop of Carlisle live out his life at a remote religious retreat, far removed from the politics of the court.

10. King Henry plans a pilgrimage to the Holy Land to absolve his guilt about King Richard's murder.

Suggested Essay Topics

1. Explore King Henry's merciful pardons of Aumerle and the Bishop of Carlisle and the ways in which they contrast with his indirect decree that he would like to see Richard dead. What reasons might King Henry have for desiring Richard's murder instead of sparing his life by sending him into exile in France?

2. Compare and contrast the mood and images of Richard's soliloquy in prison in Act V, Scene 5 with the mood and images of his long speeches in Act III, Scene 3, lines 71-99 and 142-174—the scene where he surrenders to Bolingbroke.

3. Examine the role of the women in the play.

4. Compare and contrast King Richard and Henry Bolingbroke. Does Bolingbroke seem better suited than his predecessor to the challenges of kingship?

Sample Analytical Paper Topics

The following paper topics are based on the entire play. Following each topic is a thesis and sample outline. Use these as a starting point for your paper.

Topic #1

In the first five scenes of *Richard II*, Shakespeare depicts his protagonist as a weak, capricious king with a number of less than admirable qualities. However, in later scenes Richard becomes a more sympathetic character. Write an essay that examines what we learn about King Richard's personal qualities in each of the play's five acts, focusing on the ways in which he changes and grows during the course of the play.

Outline

I. Thesis Statement: *Although Shakespeare depicts King Richard as weak and capricious in the first five scenes of* Richard II, *the King becomes a more sympathetic character during the course of the play.*

II. Act I

  A. King Richard is revealed as ineffectual when he is unable to arbitrate a quarrel between two of his noblemen

  B. In Scene 2, we learn that King Richard was responsible for the murder of his uncle, the Duke of Gloucester

C. In Scene 3, King Richard capriciously halts the trial by combat of Bolingbroke and Mowbray before it can begin and imposes unequal sentences of banishment on the adversaries; he banishes Bolingbroke for ten years and Mowbray for life

D. The King is flippant when he remarks that he has "plucked four away" from Bolingbroke's sentence, and when he tells Gaunt, "Why! uncle, thou has many years to live"

E. In Scene 4, we see King Richard mocking the banished Bolingbroke; the King also reveals that he has little concern for the common citizens of his realm

F. King Richard reveals his lack of scruples when he decides to mortgage royal lands and authorizes blank checks to be written in the names of his subjects; he is shockingly callous when he expresses the hope that his uncle, John of Gaunt, will die so he can seize his estate for the crown

III. Act II

A. In Scene 1, we learn through the conversation of Gaunt and the Duke of York that King Richard is extravagant, listens only to his flattering courtiers, and cares little for wise advice; Gaunt laments that his beloved England under Richard's reign has fallen into a perilous state of decline

B. When Gaunt, on his deathbed, scolds King Richard for ordering the Duke of Gloucester's murder and bringing England to the brink of financial ruin, the King, unable to accept criticism, becomes furious and calls his uncle a "lunatic, lean-witted fool"

C. After the news is brought of Gaunt's death, Richard, without considering the potential consequences, seizes Gaunt's estate to finance his Irish campaign, disinheriting Henry Bolingbroke

D. Richard callously ignores the Duke of York's warning that in seizing Gaunt's estate he is challenging the entire system of inheritance that made him King

E. We learn in the conversation between Northumberland, Willoughby, and Ross that Richard has been "basely led by flatterers"; we also learn that he has imposed unpopular fines and taxes on the nobles and commoners and has lost the respect and allegience of many of his countrymen

F. In Act II, Scene 2, the Queen reveals that Richard, despite his many faults, is a man who is loved and missed; her concern for her "sweet Richard" represents a turning point in the way the King is depicted and casts him in a more sympathetic light

IV. Act III

A. Richard returns to England after his Irish campaign a changed man; in Scene 2, he expresses a love of his native land

B. Confronted by a series of disasters—the loss of his Welsh army, Bolingbroke's growing strength, and the capture and execution of his favorites—Richard reveals a new dimension to his nature: he emerges as a sensitive, imaginative poet-philosopher who muses eloquently about the "death of kings" and the "hollow crown"

C. In this same speech, Richard reveals that he is an ordinary man who suffers as well as a king when he comments poignantly to his remaining supporters: "I live with bread like you, feel want,/ Taste grief, need friends" (175-176)

D. Realizing his cause is lost, Richard generously releases his remaining soldiers "To ear the land that hath some hope to grow" (212)

E. In Scene 3, King Richard, eloquent in defeat, contemplates exchanging the trappings of his kingship for an austere religious life; he anticipates martyrdom and an "obscure grave"

V. Act IV

   A. Richard, called before Parliament to formally abdicate, emphasizes his personal sorrow at being forced to renounce his throne

   B. Richard reveals defiant courage when he stresses that Bolingbroke is a traitorous usurper

   C. Although Richard carefully stage manages his abdication and reveals a keen sense of the theatrical when he passes the crown to Bolingbroke and smashes a mirror, his grief and sense of loss are genuine; he emerges as a sympathetic figure

VI. Act V

   A. In Scene 1, Richard's parting with his Queen reveals his newfound sense of humility and his genuine affection for his wife

   B. The Duke of York's tale of Richard's entry into London in Scene 2 shows that Richard had dealt courageously with his adversity

   C. Richard's soliloquy in Scene 5 reveals the former king as a poetic dreamer who has been changed for the better by his misfortunes; his experiences have brought him self-knowledge

   D. Richard attacks the men who have come to murder him, winning the admiration of Sir Pierce of Exton, who praises his valor

VII. Conclusion: Although Shakespeare, in *Richard II*, depicts King Richard as weak and unscrupulous early in the play, the King's poetic eloquence and courage in dealing with adversity establish him as a more attractive figure as the play progresses; ultimately he engages our sympathy and assumes the dimensions of a tragic hero.

Topic #2

In Act III, Scene 4 of *Richard II*, the Master Gardener comments to one of his men: "Go, bind thou up young dangling apricocks,/ Which like unruly children make their sire/ Stoop with oppression of their prodigal weight." (29-31) He thus underscores one of the thematic motifs of the play: the disparity between the values and virtues of fathers and sons. Write an essay in which you examine the differences between Edward the Black Prince and King Richard, John of Gaunt and Henry Bolingbroke, Bolingbroke and Prince Hal, and the Duke of York and the Duke of Aumerle.

Outline

I.   Thesis Statement: *Although the blood of inheritance is mentioned frequently in* Richard II, *sons are often unlike their fathers as Shakespeare reveals in his descriptions or depictions of Edward the Black Prince and King Richard, John of Gaunt and Henry Bolingbroke, Bolingbroke and Prince Hal, and the Duke of York and the Duke of Aumerle.*

II. King Richard and his father

   A.   In Act II, Scene 1, John of Gaunt refers to King Richard's illustrious ancestry several times; he comments on England's "royal kings/ Feared by their breed, and famous by their birth,/ Renownèd for their deeds" (51-53) and remarks that King Richard has disgraced his grandfather and father by his irresponsible financial policies, and by ordering the Duke of Gloucester's murder

   B.   In this same scene, the Duke of York compares King Richard to his father and tells the King he has inherited few of his father's noble qualities: "His face thou hast .../ But when he frowned it was against the French,/ And not against his friends; his noble hand/ Did win what he did spend, and spend not that/ Which his triumphant father's hand had won;/ His hands were guilty of no kindred blood,/ But bloody with the enemies of his kin" (176; 178-183)

III. John of Gaunt and Bolingbroke

A. In Act I, Scene 1, Bolingbroke reveals his rebellious nature when he defies his father by refusing to throw down the Duke of Norfolk's gage; although the father-son relationship is loving and respectful, we learn that there are significant differences between the two men

B. In Act I, Scene 2, we learn that Gaunt respects Richard's divine right to the throne; he argues that the King's actions can be reckoned with only by God, yet Bolingbroke, in the previous scene, had challenged the King by accusing him indirectly of Gloucester's murder

C. Gaunt, although saddened by his son's impending exile, respects Richard's sentence of banishment and has counseled the King as an impartial judge rather than a father; Bolingbroke, on the other hand, is bitter at his sentence and refuses to accept it philosophically as his father urges him to do

D. When he returns to England with an army, Bolingbroke reveals that he has little respect for Richard's divine right to govern; in Act I, Scene 2, Gaunt pledged that he would not lift "an angry arm" against the King, yet Bolingbroke, unlike his father, takes action when confronted by a royal injustice

IV. Bolingbroke and Prince Hal

A. In Act V, Scene 3, Bolingbroke expresses concern about his own rebellious son, Prince Hal, when he comments: "If any plague hang over us, 'tis he"; (3) Hal spends his time in taverns and brothels consorting with "loose companions" and has revealed little nobility of character

B. Bolingbroke's optimistic prediction that he sees in his son "sparks of better hope,/ Which elder years may happily bring forth" (21-22) will indeed be fulfilled, for as Shakespeare's audience knew, Prince Hal would later become the honored warrior-king Henry V

V.   The Duke of York and the Duke of Aumerle

     A.   In Act II, Scene 2, York, after learning of Bolingbroke's rebellion and discovering that his son is missing, worries that Aumerle may have enlisted in Bolingbroke's cause

     B.   In Act V, Scene 2, York tells his wife that their allegiance is now to Bolingbroke; Aumerle, however, has retained his personal allegiance to King Richard and has joined a plot to kill the new king

     C.   When York discovers a letter that implicates his son in the conspiracy, he calls Aumerle a villain and a traitor and resolves to inform King Henry of his son's role in the plot

     D.   In Act V, Scene 3, York, furious at his son's disloyalty to the crown, urges King Henry to deal harshly with Aumerle; after the King issues a royal pardon, the Duchess of York praises him but York, significantly, remains silent

VI.   Conclusion: In *Richard II*, Shakespeare reveals that sons often fail to inherit the values of their fathers. In doing so, he provides a personal note of conflict that mirrors the political issues of the play.

Topic #3

A central theme of *Richard II* is the divine right of kings. One of the principal conflicts of the play is the disparity between King Richard's erratic and unprincipled actions as sovereign and what he and many of the characters in the play regard as his divine right to govern. Write an essay in which you explore the many references in this play to the king's "divine right."

Outline

I.   Thesis Statement: T*he divine right of kings is one of the central themes in Shakespeare's* Richard II.

II.   Acts I and II

     A.   In Act I, Scene 1, King Richard refers to his "sacred blood" (119)

    B. In Scene 2, John of Gaunt tells his sister-in-law, the widowed Duchess of Gloucester, that only God can avenge her husband's death, for King Richard, "God's substitute," ordered Gloucester's murder; Gaunt respects Richard's divine right and claims he will never lift an "angry arm against [God's] minister" (37-38; 41)

    C. In Act II, Scene 3, York reminds Bolingbroke that he is rebelling against an "annointed king" (95)

III. Act III, Scene 2

    A. After King Richard returns from Ireland and learns of Bolingbroke's rebellion, the Bishop of Carlisle assures his sovereign that the "power that made you king/ Hath power to keep you king in spite of all" (27-28)

    B. King Richard proclaims soon afterward that "Not all the water in the rough rude sea/ Can wash the balm off from an annointed king;/ The breath of worldly men cannot depose/ The deputy elected by the Lord" (54-57)

    C. King Richard comments that if his subjects have rebelled, "They break their faith to God as well as us" (101)

    D. The King symbolically abandons his divinity when he tells his remaining supporters, "I live with bread like you, feel want,/ Taste grief—subjected thus,/ How can you say to me, I am a king?" (175-177)

IV. Act III, Scene 3

    A. York laments "the heavy day/ When such a sacred king should hide his head" (8-9)

    B. King Richard, confronting Northumberland from the castle walls, asserts his right to the throne by proclaiming, "Show us the hand of God/ That hath dismissed us from our stewardship" (76-77)

    C. Later in this speech, Richard tells Northumberland: "Yet know, my master, God omnipotent,/ Is mustering in his clouds on our behalf/ Armies of pestilence, and they shall strike/ Your children yet unborn and unbegot/ That lift your vassal hands against my head,/ And threat the glory of my precious crown" (84-89)

    D.   Northumberland replies that "The King of heaven forbid our lord the King/ Should so with civil and uncivil arms/ Be rushed upon" (100-102)

V.   Act IV

    A.   When Bolingbroke announces his intention to ascend "the regal throne," the Bishop of Carlisle protests, "Shall the figure of God's majesty,/ His captain, steward, deputy elect,/ Annointed, crownèd .../ Be judged by subject and inferior breath?" (125-128)

    B.   Richard, in twice comparing himself to Christ, asserts that the rejection of God's annointed is being enacted once again

    C.   Richard, although accepting his worldly circumstances, proclaims, "God save the King, although I be not he;/ And yet amen, if heaven do think him me" (174-175)

    D.   In his formal speech of abdication, Richard renounces his "sacred state" (208)

VI.   Act V

    A.   In Scene 2, The Duke of York tells his wife that heaven had a hand in Richard's deposition and Bolingbroke's accession to the throne

    B.   In Scene 3, The Duchess of York tells King Henry after he pardons her son, "A god on earth thou art" (135)

    C.   In Scene 6, Northumberland proclaims to the new king: "To thy sacred state wish I all happiness" (6)

VII. Conclusion: Although King Richard asserts his divine right to the throne many times in this play, his human failings lead to his downfall. The Duke of York speaks for many of his countrymen when he remarks that Richard's undoing was the will of heaven; by the end of the play Richard's divine right has been effectively transferred to his successor.

Topic #4

The issue of loyalty is one of the many themes explored in *Richard II*. Write an essay in which you examine the conflict between personal loyalty and loyalty to the crown as evidenced by John of Gaunt, the Duke of York, and the Duke of Aumerle.

Outline

I.   Thesis Statement: *Loyalty is one of the many themes of Shakespeare's* Richard II.

II. John of Gaunt

    A.   In Act I, Scene 2, Gaunt is shaken by the fact that King Richard had ordered the murder of his brother, the Duke of Gloucester, yet he refuses to take vengeful action because he is loyal to the King and believes he rules by divine right

    B.   In Act I, Scene 3, Gaunt further reveals his loyalty to his sovereign when he counsels the King to banish his son; he acts as an impartial judge rather than a father

    C.   In Act II, Scene 1, the dying Gaunt abandons his allegiance to the monarchy when King Richard responds callously to his criticism; he rebukes the King and tells him, "These words hereafter thy tormentors be" (136)

III. The Duke of York

    A.   In Act II, Scene 1, York criticizes Richard's seizure of his brother's estate; Richard, however, is aware of York's loyalty to the crown and appoints him Lord Governor while he is away in Ireland

    B.   In Act II, Scene 2, York reveals that his loyalties are divided between his nephews, King Richard and Bolingbroke; he is loyal to the monarchy but knows that Bolingbroke has been wronged by the King

    C.   In Act II, Scene 3, York criticizes Bolingbroke for leading an armed rebellion against the crown, but he acknowledges that Bolingbroke has been treated unfairly and pledges to remain neutral in the conflict

D. In Act III, Scene 2, we learn that York has now allied with Bolingbroke

E. In Act V, Scene 2, York, although sympathetic to King Richard, tells his wife that their loyalties now lie with Bolingbroke; he proves his allegiance to the new King by rushing to tell him that his son, the Duke of Aumerle, is involved in a treacherous plot to assassinate his sovereign

IV. The Duke of Aumerle

A. In Act I, Scene 4, Aumerle, who is cousin to both Richard and Bolingbroke, reveals that his loyalty lies firmly with the King

B. In Act III, Scene 3 (159), Aumerle further reveals his loyalty when he weeps at the thought of Richard's loss of the throne

C. At the end of Act IV, Aumerle, still loyal to Richard after his deposition, joins in a plot to assassinate the new King

D. In Act V, Scene 2, Aumerle's role in the conspiracy is exposed and his mother reveals that, unlike her husband, her loyalties lie with her only son

V. Conclusion: In *Richard II*, divided loyalties to family and crown provide one of the play's many conflicts.

Topic #5

In *Richard II*, Shakespeare utilizes rich poetic imagery. One of the most potent images is that of blood, which is used in two basic senses: the blood of kinship and inheritance, and the blood of murder and violent conflict. Less frequently, blood is used to denote a character who is "hot-blooded." This imagery helps to create an ominous atmosphere and also underscores the familial relationships in the play. Write an essay in which you explore Shakespeare's use of blood imagery in each of the play's five acts.

Outline

I.   Thesis Statement: *In* Richard II, *Shakespeare uses blood imagery to denote the blood of kinship and inheritance and the blood of murder and violent conflict.*

II. Act I, Scene 1

   A.   Scene 1 features a dozen references to "blood" and "bleeding"

   B.   Blood is used in the sense of inheritance when Bolingbroke and Mowbray refer to "high blood's royalty" (58; 71)

   C.   Blood is used in the sense of violence when Bolingbroke refers to the Duke of Gloucester's murder (103-104)

   D.   King Richard refers to the blood of inheritance when he mentions "our sacred blood" (119); he later attempts to settle the conflict between Bolingbroke and Mowbray without "letting blood" (153; 157)

III. Act 1, Scenes 2 and 3

   A.   In Scene 2, Gaunt refers to the blood of inheritance to denote a kinsman (l)

   B.   The Duchess of Gloucester also refers to the blood of inheritance when she describes her late husband and his brothers as seven vials of King Edward's "sacred blood" (12)

   C.   The Duchess evokes the blood of violence when she refers to "murder's bloody axe" (22)

   D.   In Scene 3, blood denotes kinship and inheritance when King Richard refers to his cousin Bolingbroke as "my blood," and when Bolingbroke calls his father "the earthly author of my blood" (57; 69)

   E.   King Richard refers to the blood of violent conflict when he claims that he halted the trial by combat so that "our kingdom's earth should not be soiled/ With that dear blood which it hath fosterèd" (125-126)

IV. Act II

    A. On his deathbed, Gaunt and York each evoke blood twice to censure King Richard for his role in the murder of a kinsman (II, i, 126; 131, 182-183)

    B. Northumberland refers to Bolingbroke's "noble blood" (II, i, 240)

    C. Among the omens cited by the Welsh Captain is the fact that the moon "looks bloody on the earth" (II, iv, 10)

V. Act III

    A. In Scene 1, Bolingbroke publicly accuses Bushy and Green of heinous crimes "to wash your blood/ From off my hands" before executing them (5)

    B. In Scene 2, King Richard remarks that he looks pale after learning that his Welsh soldiers have deserted because he has lost "the blood of twenty thousand men" (76)

    C. In Scene 3, Bolingbroke pledges that if Richard won't grant his demands he will "lay the summer's dust with showers of blood/ Rained from the wounds of slaughtered Englishmen (42-43)

    D. King Richard uses blood to allude to his divine right when he comments, "no hand of blood and bone/ Can gripe the sacred handle of our sceptre" (78)

    E. King Richard uses an extended reference to blood to evoke the results of the civil war he foresees if Bolingbroke usurps the throne (93-100)

    F. Northumberland, referring to Richard and Bolingbroke, mentions "the royalties of both your bloods" (106)

VI. Acts IV and V

    A. In Act V, the Bishop of Carlisle prophecies civil war if Bolingbroke is crowned: "The blood of English shall manure the ground" (137)

    B. In Act V, Scene 5, Exton remarks that he has "with the King's blood stained the King's own land" (110)

    C. In Scene 6, Bolingbroke laments, "Lords, I protest, my soul is full of woe/ That blood should sprinkle me to make me grow"; he vows to make a pilgrimage "to the Holy Land/ To wash this blood off from my guilty hand" (45-46; 49-50)

VII. Conclusion: In his frequent use of blood imagery, Shakespeare underscores the theme of inheritance and the many violent conflicts in the play.

SECTION EIGHT

Bibliography

Bloom, Harold, ed. *Modern Critical Interpretations. William Shakespeare's Richard II.* New York: Chelsea House, 1988.

Brown, John Russell. *Shakespeare's Plays in Performance.* London: Penguin, 1969.

Campbell, Oscar James and Edward G. Quinn, eds. *The Reader's Encyclopedia of Shakespeare.* New York: Crowell, 1966.

Cubeta, Paul, ed. *Twentieth Century Interpretations of Richard II.* Englewood Cliffs, N.J.: Prentice Hall, 1971.

Gielgud, John. *Stage Directions.* London: Heinemann, 1963.

Grebanier, Bernard. *Then Came Each Actor.* New York: David McKay, 1975.

Gupta, Sen. *Shakespeare's Historical Plays.* New York: Oxford University Press, 1964.

Gurr, Andrew, ed. *Richard II.* Cambridge: Cambridge University Press, 1984.

Holderness, Graham. *Penguin Critical Studies: Richard II.* London: Penguin, 1989.

Hutchison. Harold F. *The Hollow Crown: A Life of Richard II.* London: Eyre & Spottiswoode, 1961.

Kantorowicz, Ernest H. *The King's Two Bodies.* Princeton: Princeton University Press, 1957.

Kott, Jan. *Shakespeare Our Contemporary.* Trans. Boleslaw Taborski. Rev. ed. Garden City, N.Y.: Anchor Books, 1966.

Manheim, Michael. *The Weak King Dilemma in the Shakespearean History Play.* Syracuse: Syracuse University Press, 1973.

Muir, Kenneth, ed. *Richard II.* New York: Signet, 1963.

Newlin, Jeanne T., ed. *Richard II: Critical Essays.* New York: Garland, 1984.

Odell, G. C. D. *Shakespeare From Betterton to Irving.* 2 vols. New York: Scribner's, 1920.

Page, Malcolm. *Text & Performance: Richard II.* Atlantic Highlands, N.J.: Humanities Press International, 1987.

Pierce, Robert B. *Shakespeare's History Plays: The Family and the State.* Columbus: Ohio State University Press, 1971.

Prior, Moody E. *The Drama of Power.* Evanston, Ill.: Northwestern University Press, 1973.

Reese, M. M. *The Cease of Majesty.* London: Edward Arnold, 1961.

Roberts, Josephine A. *Richald II: An Annotated Bibliography.* 2 vols. New York: Garland, 1988.

Saccio, Peter. *Shakespeare's English Kings.* New York: Oxford University Press, 1977.

Schoenbaum, S. "'Richard II' and the Realities of Power." *Shakespeare Survey* 28 (1975), 1-13.

Speaight, Robert. *Shakespeare on the Stage.* Boston: Little, Brown, 1973.

Steel, Anthony. *Richard II.* Cambridge: Cambridge University Press, 1962.

Tillyard, E. M. W. *Shakespeare's History Plays.* London: Chatto & Windus, 1964.

Traversi, Derek. *Shakespeare From Richard II to Henry V.* London: Hollis & Carter, 1958.

Weiss, Theodore. *The Breath of Clowns and Kings.* New York: Athenium, 1971.

Wells, Stanley, ed. *William Shakespeare: A Bibliographical Guide.* Rev. ed. Oxford: Oxford University Press, 1990.

Winny, James. *The Player King.* New York: Barnes & Noble, 1968.

The High School Tutors

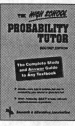
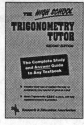

THE BEST TEST PREPARATION FOR THE

SAT II: Subject Test

LITERATURE

by Joseph A. Alvarez, Ph.D. • Pauline Beard, Ph.D. • Ellen Davis, M.A. • Philip Harmon, Ph.D.

6 Full-Length Exams

➤ Every question based on the current exams
➤ The ONLY test preparation book with detailed explanations to every question
➤ Far more comprehensive than any other test preparation book

Includes a Comprehensive **COURSE REVIEW** of Literature, emphasizing all areas of literature found on the exam

Research & Education Association

Available at your local bookstore or order directly from us by sending in coupon below.

REA's Test Preps
The Best in Test Preparation

- REA "Test Preps" are far **more** comprehensive than any other test preparation series
- Each book contains up to **eight** full-length practice exams based on the most recent exams
- **Every** type of question likely to be given on the exams is included
- Answers are accompanied by **full** and **detailed** explanations

REA has published over 60 Test Preparation volumes in several series. They include:

Advanced Placement Exams (APs)
Biology
Calculus AB & Calculus BC
Chemistry
Computer Science
English Language & Composition
English Literature & Composition
European History
Government & Politics
Physics
Psychology
Spanish Language
United States History

**College Level Examination
   Program (CLEP)**
American History I
Analysis & Interpretation of
   Literature
College Algebra
Freshman College Composition
General Examinations
Human Growth and Development
Introductory Sociology
Principles of Marketing

SAT II: Subject Tests
American History
Biology
Chemistry
French
German
Literature

SAT II: Subject Tests (continued)
Mathematics Level IC, IIC
Physics
Spanish
Writing

Graduate Record Exams (GREs)
Biology
Chemistry
Computer Science
Economics
Engineering
General
History
Literature in English
Mathematics
Physics
Political Science
Psychology
Sociology

ACT - American College Testing
   Assessment

ASVAB - Armed Service Vocational
   Aptitude Battery

CBEST - California Basic Educational
   Skills Test

CDL - Commercial Driver's License Exam

CLAST - College Level Academic Skills
   Test

ELM - Entry Level Mathematics

ExCET - Exam for Certification of
   Educators in Texas

FE (EIT) - Fundamentals of
   Engineering Exam

FE Review - Fundamentals of
   Engineering Review

GED - High School Equivalency
   Diploma Exam (US & Canadian
   editions)

GMAT - Graduate Management
   Admission Test

LSAT - Law School Admission Test

MAT - Miller Analogies Test

MCAT - Medical College Admission
   Test

MSAT - Multiple Subjects
   Assessment for Teachers

NTE - National Teachers Exam

PPST - Pre-Professional Skills Tests

PSAT - Preliminary Scholastic
   Assessment Test

SAT I - Reasoning Test

SAT I - Quick Study & Review

TASP - Texas Academic Skills
   Program

TOEFL - Test of English as a
   Foreign Language

RESEARCH & EDUCATION ASSOCIATION
61 Ethel Road W. • Piscataway, New Jersey 08854
Phone: (908) 819-8880

Please send me more information about your Test Prep Books

Name _____

Address _____

City _____ State _____ Zip _____

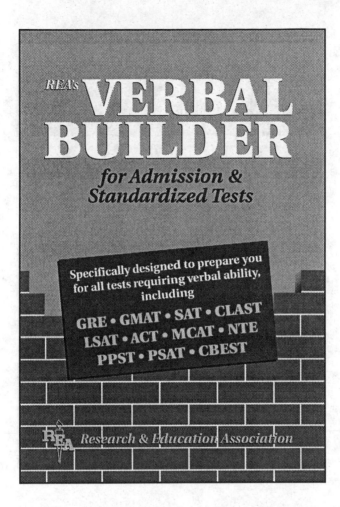